The Letters of Amerigo Vespucci

Documents of his Discoveries, Exploration and Mapping of the New World and South Americas

Translated by Clements R. Markham

Published by Pantianos Classics

ISBN-13: 978-1-78987-066-4

First published in 1894

Contents

Introduction

The account of the alleged voyage of Amerigo Vespucci in 1497-98 was written for that worthy's own countrymen, and for foreigners who lived at a distance from the Peninsula. When, after some years, the story reached Spain in print, men were still alive who would have known whether any such voyage had ever been made. Among them was the able and impartial historian Las Casas, who considered that the story was false, and disproved it from internal evidence. The authority of Las Casas is alone conclusive. Modern investigators, such as Robertson, Muñoz, Navarrete, Humboldt, Washington Irving, and D'Avezac examined the question, and they all came to the same conclusion as Las Casas.

The matter appeared to be finally settled until 1865. In that year M. F. de Varnhagen, Baron of Porto Seguro in Brazil, published a book at Lima, 1 where he was accredited as Brazilian Minister, with the object of rehabilitating the Florentine's character for honesty, by arguing that the story of the alleged voyage in 1497-98 was worthy of credit. This makes it desirable that the whole question should once more be discussed. Varnhagen at least deserves the thanks of all students of the history of American discovery for having published, in an accessible form, both the Latin and the Italian texts of the letters of Vespucci.

It has been decided by the Council of the Hakluyt Society to supply a volume to the members containing translations of the letters of Vespucci, of the chapters in which they are discussed in the history of Las Casas, and other original documents relating to the subject. Readers will thus be enabled to form independent judgments on this vexed question; while the Introduction will furnish them with the events of the life of Vespucci, and with a review of the arguments in support of Varnhagen's theory, as well as of those which militate against it.

A Life of Vespucci was published by an enthusiastic fellow-countryman named Bandini, in 1745, 2 who collected all there is to be known respecting his family and early life at Florence, and reprinted his authentic letters. Canovai was another biographer, and a still warmer panegyrist. 3

There are three spurious letters attributed to Vespucci, but they are now so universally held to be forgeries, that they need not occupy our time. 4

We learn from Bandini that Amerigo was the third son of a notary at Florence, named Ser Nastagio (Anastasio) Vespucci, by Lisabetta Mini, and that he was born on March 9th, 1451. 5 He was thus four years younger than Columbus. Amerigo studied under his uncle, Fra Giorgio Antonio Vespucci, a Dominican monk of St. Marco, at Florence, who taught him Latin. A letter from Amerigo to his father, in Latin, has been preserved, dated on October 18th, 1476, at Mugello, near Trebbio, whither he had been sent in consequence of an epidemic then raging at Florence. In the same year the elder brother, Antonio, was sent to the University of Pisa. He was a scholar and an author. His eldest son, Bartolomeo, rose to be Professor of Astrology at Pisa, and left a son. His second son, Giovanni, eventually joined his uncle Amerigo in Spain, and became a pilot. The other brother, Geronimo, went as a merchant to Syria, where he lost all he had made after nine years of labour. This is stated in a letter to Amerigo, dated July 24th, 1489, which was brought to Italy by a priest named Carnesecchi, who was returning.

Amerigo Vespucci embraced a mercantile life at Florence, 6 and was eventually taken into the great commercial house of the Medici, the head of which was Lorenzo Piero Francesco di Medici, who succeeded his father, Lorenzo the Magnificent, in 1492. The house had transactions in Spain, and required experienced agents at Cadiz. Amerigo, who was then over forty years of age, and Donato Niccolini were selected for this duty, and took up their residence at Cadiz and Seville in 1492. In December 1495, an Italian merchant, named Juanoto Berardi, died at Seville, and Vespucci was employed to wind up his affairs. This Berardi had contracted, on April 9th, 1495, to supply the Government with twelve vessels of 900 tons each for the Indies. 7 He handed over the first four in the same April, four more in June, and the rest in September, but unluckily the four last were wrecked before delivery. 8 On the 10th of April 1495, the Spanish Government broke faith with Columbus, and contrary to the concession made to him, free navigation was allowed to the Indies, on condition that the ships sailed from Cadiz, and were registered as submitting to certain engagements as regards the State. Gomara, an unreliable authority, alleges that many vessels took advantage of this concession. It is likely enough that some were sent on commercial ventures, but it is grossly improbable that any discoveries of importance were made and left entirely unrecorded. The Admiral remonstrated against the infraction of his rights, and the order of April 10th, 1495, was cancelled on June 2nd, 1497.

During this period Vespucci was engaged at Cadiz as a provision contractor. A record is preserved of his having received 10,000 maravedis from Treasurer Pinelo on January 12th, 1496, for payment of sailors' wages; and we learn from Muñoz that other entries 9 prove that Vespucci continued his business of provision merchant at least until May 1498. He contracted for one, if not for two, of the expeditions of Columbus. A very civil and plausible man was this beef contractor, and the Admiral spoke of him, seven years afterwards, as being very respectable (hombre muy de bien).

In 1499, the very respectable contractor, who was approaching the age of fifty, determined to retire from business and go to sea. His own reasons for this complete change in his old age were that he had already seen and known various changes of fortune in business; that a man might at one time be at the top of the well and at another be fallen and subject to losses; and that it had become evident to him that a merchant's life was one of continual labour, with the chance of failure and ruin. It was rather late in life to make these discoveries, and it may fairly be suspected that there was some more concrete reason for his change of life which he concealed under these generalities.

The expedition in which Vespucci sailed was organised and fitted out by Alonzo de Hojeda in 1499. Columbus, having discovered the island of Trinidad and the mainland of South America on the 31st of July 1498, arrived at San Domingo in the end of August. In October he sent five ships to Spain with the news of the discovery, a chart of the new coast-line and islands, and a report containing mention of the existence of pearls. These precious documents fell into the hands of Bishop Fonseca, who showed them to Hojeda, a man whom he favoured. The Bishop suggested that his protégé should equip an expedition to reap all the advantages to be derived from the discoveries of the Admiral, and granted him a licence. Hojeda was nothing loth, but he was in want of funds, and only succeeded in fitting out four vessels by promising shares of the expected profits to persons in Seville and Cadiz who would advance money. Vespucci seems to have been one of these promoters of Hojeda's voyage. Las Casas supposes that he was taken on board as a merchant who had contributed to the expenses, and also possibly on account of his theoretical knowledge of cosmography, of which he doubtless made the most.

As there is no doubt that Vespucci wrote the famous letters from Lisbon, we may gather some idea of the man from their contents. He was fond of airing his classical knowledge, though it was a mere smattering; for he thought that Pliny was the contemporary of Mecænas, 10 and that the sculptor Policletus was a painter. 11 On the other hand he quotes Petrarch, and gives a correct reference to a passage in Dante's Inferno. 12 He was inaccurate in his narratives and regardless of the truth, as was ably shown by Las Casas, 13 while he habitually assumed the credit of work which belonged to his superiors; and pretended to knowledge and influence which he could never have possessed. 14 Though externally civil and obliging, he harboured jealousy and hatred in his heart, 15 and was disloyal towards the men under whom he served. 16 Of his natural ability there can be no doubt. He wrote well, and some of his stories are capitally told. 17 He must have been a plausible talker, so that, by such men as Fonseca and Peter Martyr, the theoretical pretender was taken at the value he put upon himself, and was believed to be a great pilot and navigator. 18

He was certainly not a practical navigator, much less a pilot, as the term was understood in those days. Hojeda, in his evidence, said that he took with him "Juan de la Cosa, and Morigo Vespuche, and other pilots". In this sentence the "other pilots" must be intended to be coupled with Juan de la Cosa, not with "Morigo Vespuche". A man of fifty years of age could not go to sea for the first time and be a pilot. The thing would be absurd now, but it would be much more absurd in the fifteenth century. With the perfectly graduated and adjusted instruments, the facilities for calculations, and the appliances of all kinds with which the modern navigator is supplied, the business of the sea may be learnt more quickly than in former days. Yet no one would now dream of calling a middle-aged man an expert navigator because he had read a book on astronomy and made one or two voyages. In the fifteenth century the instruments were of the roughest kind, and much more depended on the skill and intuitive instincts of the seaman himself, qualifications which could only be acquired by a long training and many years of experience. Vespucci has the assurance to talk of his astrolabe and quadrant and sea chart, and to write disparagingly of the trained pilots of whom he was jealous. 19 But his own writings make it clear to any seaman that the Florentine contractor was merely a landlubber with a smattering of Sacrobosco or some other work De Sphæra, which enabled him to impose upon his brother landsmen by talking of climates, of steering by winds, and of measuring diameters of fixed stars. Hojeda certainly did not ship a pilot when he took Amerigo Vespucci on board, but a very clever and very plausible landsman with a keen eye to his own interests.

Alonzo de Hojeda left Cadiz, with four vessels, on May 20th, 1499. Endeavouring to steer by the chart of Columbus, he made a landfall at some distance to the south of Paria, off the mouths of the Orinoco. Coasting along to the northward, he came to the Gulf of Paria, went out by the Boca del Drago, and visited the island of Margarita. He then proceeded along the coast of the continent, visited Curaçoa, which he called the "Isla de los Gigantes", and came to the Gulf of Maracaibo, where he found a village built on piles, which was named Venezuela, or Little Venice. His most western point was the province of Cuquibacoa and the Cabo de la Vela. His discovery consisted of 200 leagues of coast to the west of Paria. Along this coast Hojeda obtained gold and pearls. He had an encounter with the natives, in which one Spaniard was killed and about twenty wounded, the place being named "Puerto Flechado". He refitted in a harbour where the people were friendly, and which Amerigo considered to be the best harbour in the world. Las Casas believed this to have been Cariaco, near Cumana. On leaving the coast Hojeda proceeded to Española, where he behaved in the outrageous manner described by Las Casas, 20 remaining two months and seventeen days, from September 5th, 1499, to November 22nd, finally visiting some islands, probably the Bahamas, 21 and carrying off 200 natives as slaves. Hojeda returned to Cadiz in February 1500. In the same year Juan de la Cosa, the pilot of the expedition, compiled his famous map of the world, on which he delineated this new coast-line from Paria to Cabo de la Vela, the extreme point of continental land that was known up to that time. On this coast-line he placed twenty-two names, including the Boca del Drago, Margarita, the "Isla de los Gigantes", the Lake of Venezuela (or Little Venice), and the Cabo de la Vela. The map of Juan de la Cosa is important when we come to the consideration of the statements in the letters of Vespucci.

The Florentine, on his return from this voyage, took up his residence at Seville. Here, according to his own account, he received a message from the King of Portugal, asking him to come to Lisbon. The bearer of the message was a countryman of his own, named Giuliano di Bartolomeo di Giocondo, and Vespucci would have us believe that the King attached importance to his entering the Portuguese service. The Visconde de Santarem has searched the archives in the Torre do Tombo at Lisbon, and all the Portuguese documents in Paris, without once meeting with the name of Vespucci. This absence of all official allusion to him points to the conclusion that he never held any important position as pilot or commander. He asserts that he joined a Portuguese expedition of discovery along the coast of Brazil, which sailed on March 10th, 1501, and returned on September 7th, 1502. 22 In the following March or April (1503) he addressed a letter to the head of the mercantile house to which he had belonged, Lorenzo Piero Francesco di Medici, giving his account of the voyage. On May 10th, 1503, he sailed from Lisbon on another voyage, returning on June 28th, 1504.

In the following September he finished writing the famous letter containing an account of his alleged four voyages. The original Italian version was sent to a magnificent Lord, who is supposed to have been Piero Soderini, Gonfaloniere of Florence in 1504; and a French translation was sent to Renè, Duke of Lorraine. Soon afterwards Vespucci left the Portuguese service and returned to Spain.

In February 1505, the Admiral, Christopher Columbus, was laid up with an illness at Seville, while his brother and his son Diego were at court. Vespucci, having returned to Spain from Lisbon, went to pay his respects to the great discoverer, and the Admiral entrusted him with a letter to his son. "The bearer of this letter", wrote Columbus, "is going to court on matters relating to navigation. He always showed a desire to please me, and he is a very respectable man. Fortune has been adverse to him, as to many others. His labours have not been so profitable to him as might have been expected. He leaves me with the desire to do me service, if it should be in his power." Vespucci had evidently been complaining to the Admiral that his Portuguese service had been a failure, and had brought him no profit. He went on to the court of Ferdinand, and soon obtained employment; receiving letters of naturalisation on the 24th of April 1505 23; but there is no record of his ever having been of any service to the Admiral. He was very plausible, and knew how to ingratiate himself with men in power. It was intended to send him on a voyage of discovery with Vicente Yañez Pinzon, and in 1506 and 1507 he was engaged in purchasing provisions for the voyage; but the idea of despatching this expedition was abandoned in 1508. 24

It has been supposed, from a sentence in a letter from Hieronimo Vianelo, the Venetian Ambassador, dated at Burgos on December 23rd, 1506, that

Vespucci accompanied Juan de la Cosa on a voyage of discovery to the Indies during that year. 25 "The two ships have arrived from the Indies which went on a voyage of discovery under Juan Biscaino and Almerigo Fiorentino." But Vianelo must have been misinformed. There are documentary proofs that Vespucci was in Spain until August 1506. It is highly probable that the voluble Florentine retailed the story of Juan de la Cosa's voyage in such a way as to give Vianelo the impression that the narrator took part in it himself. The story of the voyage, as we find it in the letter of the Venetian Ambassador, is quite in Vespucci's manner.

On the 6th of August 1508, Amerigo Vespucci received the appointment of Chief Pilot (Piloto Mayor) of Spain, with a salary of 75,000 maravedis a year. 26 The "Real Titulo", or commission, is a curious and very interesting document. He is ordered to prepare an authoritative chart, called a "Padron General", on which all discoveries are to be shown, and whence the charts for all ships are to be copied; and he is also to examine all pilots in the use of the astrolabe and quadrant, and to give instruction in his house at Seville. Vespucci was able to give theoretical instruction in cosmography; although a man who first went to sea when he was nearly fifty, and who had only made three voyages, could not be an experienced pilot. With such experts as Juan de la Cosa, Juan Diaz de Solis, Vicente Pinzon, and others, available, it was indeed a strange selection. But Ferdinand and Fonseca were notorious for their bad appointments. Columbus was sent home in chains, Blasco Nuñez de Balboa was beheaded; while high places, for which they were more or less unfit, were entrusted to Ovando, Bobadilla, Pedrarias, and Vespucci.

Vespucci held the appointment of Chief Pilot until the 22nd of February 1512, when he died at Seville, aged 61. He had married a Spaniard named Maria Cerezo, but left no children. His widow received a pension of 10,000 maravedis, 27 to be paid out of the salary of her husband's successor, 28 Juan Diaz de Solis. Vespucci left his papers to his nephew Giovanni, son of his brother Antonio, who received the appointment of a royal pilot, with a salary of 20,000 maravedis, on May 22nd, 1512. 29 He went as chief pilot in the expedition of Pedrarias Davila in 1514; and is mentioned as a royal pilot in 1515 and 1516. In 1524 he was a member of the Badajoz Commission, but was dismissed in March 1525.

This is all that is known of the life of Amerigo Vespucci, beyond what is contained in his own letters, which we will now proceed to consider in detail.

Of the two letters of Vespucci that have been preserved, the earliest was written from Lisbon in March or April 1503, and was addressed to Lorenzo Piero Francesco di Medici. The original Italian text is lost, but it was translated into Latin by "Jocundus Interpreter", who is supposed to have been the same Giuliano di Bartolomeo di Giocondo who brought the invitation to Vespucci to come to Portugal in 1501. 30 The letter describes the voyage of discovery sent from Lisbon in May 1501, in which Vespucci alleged that he took part. He alludes to a previous letter in which he had fully described "the new countries", and continues: "it is lawful to call it a new world, because none of these countries were known to our ancestors, and to all who hear about them they will be entirely new." He does not mention the name of the commander of the expedition, and assumes all the glory of the discovery for himself. "I have found a continent in that southern part more populous and more full of animals than our Europe or Asia or Africa." 31 Moreover, the safety of the ships, their navigation across the ocean, their escape from perils, were all due to this wonderful beef contractor, if we are to believe his own account. "If my companions had not trusted in me, to whom cosmography was known, no one, not the leader of our navigation, would have known where we were after running five hundred leagues." He goes on to tell us that his "knowledge of the marine chart, and the rules taught by it, were more worth than all the pilots in the world". 32 After relating some fictitious stories about the natives and their cannibalism, and giving a glowing but vague account of the vegetation, he concludes with some absurd remarks about the stars of the southern hemisphere, which he has the assurance to tell us were measured by him to see which was the largest. The letter concludes with the statement that this was his third voyage, as he had made two by order of the King of Spain. This is the first intimation of a design to make two voyages out of the Hojeda expedition, one of which was to precede the Admiral's discovery of the mainland. He also announces his intention of collecting all the wonderful things he had seen into a cosmographical book, that his record may live with future generations, intending to complete it, with the aid of friends, at home. The letter shows the character of the man, and how little reliance can be placed on his statements.

The letter to Medici was printed very soon after it was written. The first issue, entitled Mundus Novus, consisting of four 4to leaves, and the second, Epistola Albericij de Novo Mundo, are without place or date. A copy of the third, printed at Augsburg in 1504, and entitled Mundus Novus, is in the Grenville Library. Then followed two others, and the sixth issue was the early Paris edition of Jean Lambert, a copy of which is in the Bibliothèque Nationale. Another Paris edition, nearly as old, is in the Grenville Library. In 1505, an issue, entitled De Ora Antarctica, and edited by Ringmann, appeared at Strasbourg. The letter was also included in the book of voyages, Paesi novamente retrovati, printed at Vicenza in 1507, where it was called Novo Mondo da Alb. Vesputio. It was thus widely circulated over Europe, and Vespucci obtained the credit of discoveries made by the unnamed Portuguese commander. The title, Novus Mundus, is taken from the opening boast of his letter, that it is lawful to call the discovery a new world because no one had ever seen it before. It was thus that Vespucci got his name connected, throughout Europe, with the discovery of a New World, and this prepared the way for the proposal to give it the name of America!

The more important letter of Vespucci, containing the account of his alleged four voyages, was written in September 1504, a short time before he left Portugal. A copy, in French, was sent to René II, Duke of Lorraine, while the Italian original was addressed to a "Magnificent Lord", who is supposed, with much probability, to have been Piero Soderini, the Gonfaloniere of Florence from 1502 to 1512. Vespucci speaks of him as having been his schoolfellow, and as being, at the time the letter was written, in a high official position at Florence.

The French copy was translated into Latin, and published at St. Dié in April 1507, in the Cosmographiæ Introductio, a rare little book by the Professor of Cosmography at the University of St. Dié in Lorraine, named Martin Waldzeemüller, who used the nom de plume of Hylacomylus. The Italian version was also printed at an early date, a little volume in quarto of thirty-two pages, without place or year. It is excessively rare, only four copies being known to exist. One belonged to Baccio Valori, and from it Bandini published a new edition in 1745. It was afterwards the property of the Marchese Gino Capponi. The second belonged to Gaetano Poggiale of Leghorn, and is now in the Palatine Library at Florence. The third is in the Grenville Library. The fourth belonged to the Carthusian Monastery at Seville, and was bought by Varnhagen in 1863 at Havanna. 33

The Medici letter, and both the Latin and Italian versions of the Soderini letter, are given by Varnhagen in his work on Vespucci.

There are forty-four words or expressions of Spanish or Portuguese origin in the Italian version, 34 which Vespucci must have got into the habit of using during his long residence in Spain, even when writing in his own language. Twelve of these refer to things belonging to the sea or ships, 35 an indication that Vespucci was ignorant of maritime affairs before he went to sea with Hojeda in 1499. But the Hispanicisms also show that the letter to Soderini was written by an Italian who had lived for several years among Spaniards. Vespucci answers to this description. He had been ten years in Spain or Portugal, or in Spanish or Portuguese ships, when he composed the letter to Soderini.

The feature in Vespucci's letters that has struck nearly all the students who have examined them, is their extraordinary vagueness. Not a single name of a commander is mentioned, and in the account of the two Spanish voyages there are not half-a-dozen names of places. The admirers of Vespucci explain this away by pointing out that he was corresponding with a friend, and only wrote what was likely to amuse him; and that he refers to a book he had written for fuller details. This might explain many omissions, but it is scarcely sufficient to account for the absolute silence respecting commanders and comrades, whom it would be as natural to mention as dates or the number of ships, and quite as entertaining. This extraordinary silence can really be accounted for only by the assumption that no real names could be made to fit into the facts as he gave them. This is, no doubt, the true explanation.

The "book" is referred to in four places in the Soderini letter, and once in the Medici letter. In one place Vespucci says: "In these four voyages I have seen so many things different from our customs that I have written a book to be called The Four Voyages, in which I have related the greater part of the things that I saw, very clearly and to the best of my ability. I have not yet published it, because my own affairs are in such a bad state that I have no taste for what I have written, yet I am inclined to publish it. In this work will be seen every event in detail, so I do not enlarge upon them here." 36 A little further on he says: "In each of my voyages I have noted down the most re-markable things, and all is reduced to a volume, in the geographical style, entitled The Four Voyages, in which all things are described in detail; but I have not yet sent out a copy, because it is necessary for me to revise it." 37 According to these two statements the book had been actually written, but not yet revised or shown to anyone. He also speaks of his observations of fixed stars as being in his Four Voyages. 38 But towards the end of the letter he says that he refrains from recounting certain events, because he reserves them for his Four Voyages; and in the Medici letter he speaks of "completing his work in consultation with learned persons and aided by friends, when he should return home." 39 From these passages the most probable conclusion is, that this book was never actually written, but that Vespucci intended to write such a work when he retired to Florence. He, however, never returned home. He went to Spain and obtained lucrative employment there, and the idea of writing a book was abandoned. He would not have dared to publish the story of his first voyage in a country where the truth was well known.

The statement made by Vespucci respecting his alleged first voyage is as follows: He says that an expedition of discovery was sent by the King, con-sisting of four ships, and that the King chose him to go with it. He does not mention the name of the commander of the expedition, nor of any of the cap-tains or pilots; but he asserts that he was away eighteen months, and that he discovered a great extent of mainland and an infinite number of islands. The ships, he alleges, sailed from Cadiz on the 10th of May 1497, and proceeded to Grand Canary, which he says is in 37° 30' N. lat., and 280 leagues from Lis-bon. Thence they sailed for thirty-seven days on a W.S.W. course, making 1,000 leagues, when they reached the coast of the mainland in latitude 16° N., and longitude from Canary 70° W.

He describes the manners and customs of the people in considerable de-tail, and enumerates the animals, giving a particular account of the iguana, but without giving the animal a name. He also tells us that the native names for their different kinds of food are Yuca, Casabi, and Ignami; and that the word for a man of great wisdom is Carabi. He describes a village with forty-four large huts built over the water on poles, like a little Venice.

After sailing for eighty leagues along the coast he came to another prov-ince, of which he gives the name. It is Parias in the Latin version, but in the Italian version L has been substituted for P, and a b for s, so that the word becomes Lariab. Then comes the audacious assertion to which all this was leading. He says that he sailed along the coast, always on a N.W. course, for 870 leagues. At the end of this marvellous voyage he came to "the finest harbour in the world", where he found a friendly people, and remained to refit for thirty-seven days. Here the natives complained that they were subject to attacks from savage people who came from islands at a distance of about 100 leagues to the east. The Spaniards agreed to chastise the islanders, and after sailing N.E. and E. for 100 leagues they came to islands where the natives were called Iti. They had an encounter with them, in which one Spaniard was killed and twenty-two were wounded. But they took 222 prisoners, and sold them as slaves when they returned to Cadiz on October 15th, 1498.

Vespucci's account of the second voyage is that the expedition, consisting of three ships, sailed from Cadiz on May 16th, 1499, and stopped some days at the island of Fuoco. They then crossed the ocean after a voyage of forty-four days, going over 500 leagues on a S.W. course. The landfall was in 5° S., and the country was inundated by the mouths of a great river. They then steered north, and came to an excellent port formed by a large island. He describes the chase of a canoe, manned by cannibal people called Cambali; and the intercourse with inhabitants who told them about the pearl fishery.

They next landed on an island, fifteen leagues from the land, where the inhabitants, for want of water, chewed a green herb mixed with white powder. Leaving this island, they came to another where the people were so tall that it was named the Island of the Giants. They continued to sail along the coast, having many encounters with the natives. They found the latitude to be 15° N., and here they came to a harbour for repairing their ships, where the inhabitants were very friendly. They remained forty-seven days, and collected many pearls. Departing from this port, they shaped a course for Antiglia (Española), where they obtained supplies, remaining two months and seventeen days. Here, he says, they endured many dangers and troubles from the same Christians who were in this island with Columbus, and he believed this was caused by envy. They left the island on the 22nd of July, and, after a voyage of a month and a half, they returned to Cadiz on the 8th of September, the year not given.

Las Casas, giving Vespucci credit for two voyages, seems to have thought that he might have been with Hojeda again on his second voyage from 1502 to 1504. But Vespucci asserts that he was in Portugal, or serving on board Portuguese ships, during the whole of that period.

The first voyage appears, both from internal and external evidence, to be imaginary. The second voyage is the first of Hojeda inaccurately told, while two or three incidents of the Hojeda voyage are transferred to the imaginary first voyage. The assertion that the King sent an expedition of discovery, consisting of four ships, in May 1497, is not corroborated. There is no record of any such expedition, and there is much collateral evidence, which will be discussed further on, that no expedition was despatched by the King in that year. If such a royal expedition had been despatched, with such marvellous results, Las Casas could not have been ignorant of the fact. It has been suggested that four out of twelve ships supplied to the King by Juanato Berardi might have been used for this expedition, and that its despatch is not impossible, because May 10th, 1497, the date of sailing given by Vespucci, is previous to June 2nd, 1497, the date of the royal order cancelling permission for private ships to go to the Indies. But the alleged expedition was sent by the King, and was not a private one. It is more likely that Vespucci purposely selected a date previous to June 2nd.

The voyage across the Atlantic to the mainland, in 16° N., is described by Vespucci as having been performed in thirty-seven days, with a W.S.W. course, and a distance of 1,000 leagues. Such a course and distance would have taken him to the Gulf of Paria, not to a coast in latitude 16° N. Even with a course direct to that point, and disregarding the intervening land, the distance he gives would leave him 930 miles short of the alleged position. No actual navigator would have made such a blunder. He was quoting the reckoning from Hojeda's voyage, and invented the latitude at random. When he came to his second voyage, to make a difference, he halved the distance, saying that he was forty-four days going 500 leagues on a S.W. course. He also gives 15° as the latitude of the coast discovered when he was with Hojeda, though no part of that coast is north of 13°. His crowning statement that, starting from 23° N., he went 870 leagues along a coast always on a N.W. course, is still more preposterous. Such a course and distance would have taken him right across the continent of North America into British Columbia.

Varnhagen accepts the Florentine's latitudes, and assumes that when in 23° N. he was near Tampico, on the coast of Mexico. But he rejects the impossible courses and distances of Vespucci, substituting an imaginary voyage of his own, by which he takes our contractor along the coast of North America, round the peninsula of Florida, and up to Cape Hatteras, where, he confesses, "the finest harbour in the world" is not to be found. But such a voyage is a pure assumption, and as a serious argument it is quite inadmissible. The evidence is the other way. The latitudes are wrong, judging from the one latitude given by the Florentine in his second voyage, while the courses and distances might be relied upon as roughly correct if they were given by an honest man. Their absurdity proves the imposture.

From "the best harbour in the world" Vespucci says that he went eastward for 100 leagues to some very populous islands called Iti, where the people, after severe fighting, were defeated by the Spaniards, 222 being carried off as slaves. Having brought his protégé to Cape Hatteras, Varnhagen would identify Iti with Bermuda. But there were no natives on Bermuda when it was discovered, and no indications that it had ever been inhabited. The islands where this wholesale kidnapping took place, if the story has any foundation in fact, were probably the Windward Islands or the Bahamas, visited by Hojeda with this object after he left St. Domingo. The word Iti appears to have been an invention of Vespucci: perhaps he was thinking of the old Italian form Iti ("gone")—which he uses in its proper sense in his second voyage—or of Hayti, the native name for Española.

There are two, or perhaps three, incidents in the story of the alleged first voyage which happened in the voyage when Vespucci was with Hojeda. The first is the village built on piles over the water. Such a village was discovered by Hojeda at the entrance of the Gulf of Maracaibo, and called Little Venice, or Venezuela. Vespucci describes exactly the same thing in his first voyage, but does not mention it in his second (or Hojeda) voyage. He took it out of the real voyage in order to embellish the imaginary one. Varnhagen argues that there might easily have been two villages built on piles. But that is not the point. The point is, that there is no mention of the fact in its proper place, while it occurs in this imaginary voyage in a way that points unmistakably to the source whence it came. Then there is "the best harbour in the world", where there were friendly natives, and where the ships were refitted, the duration of the stay being given as thirty-seven days in the first, and forty-four days in the second voyage; evidently the same incident, serving for the imaginary as well as for the real voyage. This "best harbour in the world" was, according to Las Casas, the Gulf of Cariaco, near Cumana, where Hojeda refitted. Lastly, there is the encounter with natives, when one Spaniard was killed and twenty-two wounded. Vespucci asserts that an encounter took place during his first voyage with this number of casualties. Las Casas had seen a letter from Roldan, containing information from Hojeda's officers, in which an encounter is mentioned with the same casualties, one killed and about twenty wounded. Modern critics will agree with Las Casas that this coincidence is alone sufficient to prove the fictitious character of the first voyage of Vespucci.

The greater part of Vespucci's narrative of his first voyage is taken up with accounts of the manners and customs of the natives; touching which Las Casas has made some very pertinent remarks. Many of the things Vespucci states could not have been known to him in the few days that he remained on the coast, because he did not know a single word of the language, as he himself confesses. He can only be believed in those statements based on what he actually saw or might have seen, and all these are perfectly applicable to the natives of the coast seen during Hojeda's voyage. The rest are pronounced by Las Casas to be all fiction; as well as his enumeration of the animals he saw. Vespucci gives one word in the native language—Carabi, meaning "a man of great wisdom". Upon this Las Casas remarks that the Spaniards did not even know the names for bread or for water, yet Vespucci wants us to believe that, during the few days he remained at that place, he understood that Carabi signified a man of great wisdom. He got the word, of course, from the name of the people he heard of during the voyage of Hojeda—the Carribs, or Canibas—and made it serve his purpose in this passage. 40

Vespucci does not mention the names of the commanders of the expedition, nor of any of his Spanish comrades; and he gives only one native word, Carabi; three names of articles of food, Yuca, Casabi, and Ignami; and two names of places, Iti and Parias (or Lariab?).

Two of the names for food, Yuca and Casabi, belong to the language of the Antilles, and Vespucci would have heard of them during his voyage with Hojeda. Ignami is an African word, which he would have picked up at Lisbon. The use of the word Yuca, as belonging to the language of the natives of the Mexican coast near 23° N., is one more proof of the imposture of his narrative. 41

The name of Parias requires fuller notice. It is alleged to be the name of a province in 23° N., and is thus spelt in the Latin version. Las Casas, therefore, naturally used it as one argument against the truth of Vespucci's narrative, for Paria was well known to be a province of the mainland opposite the island of Trinidad, discovered by Columbus. But in the Italian version the word is Lariab, an L being substituted for P, and b for s. Varnhagen endeavours to make a strong point of this discrepancy. He eagerly adopts Lariab as the correct form, having found (not Lariab) but two words ending in ab in a vocabulary of the Huasteca Indians, whose country is near the northern frontier of Mexico. It is impossible to ascertain, with certainty, whether Parias, or Lariab, or either, was the word in the original manuscript of Vespucci, which is lost. It is in favour of Lariab that the Italian version was probably printed from the manuscript without previous translation; while the version containing Parias was translated into French, and then into Latin, before it was printed. On the other hand, there is strong reason for the belief that the editor of the Latin version had not then heard of the particulars of the third voyage of Columbus, or of the name of Paria. 42 In that case it could not have come into his head to print Parias for Lariab, and consequently Parias was the original form, and Lariab a misprint of the Italian version. On the whole, Parias is probably correct; but the question is not important, because the evidence against Vespucci is quite sufficient without the Parias argument.

The internal evidence against the authenticity of the first voyage is conclusive. It satisfied the impartial and acute historian Las Casas at the time, and has not been shaken by the arguments of Varnhagen, who did not adduce any new facts. But the external evidence is even stronger. It was evident to Varnhagen that it was a necessity of his argument that an expedition should be provided, with which Vespucci might have sailed. Without vessels and a commander there could have been no voyage. These essentials have been furnished by the rehabilitator of Vespucci with some audacity. It was recorded by Las Casas and Herrera that, after the return of Columbus from his last voyage in 1505, an expedition to follow up his discoveries was fitted out by Vicente Yañez Pinzon, Juan Diaz de Solis, and Pedro de Ledesma, and that they discovered the coast of Yucatan. Herrera gives the date 1506; but the real date was 1508, as given by Peter Martyr. 43 The authority for the narratives of Las Casas and Herrera is the evidence given by Pinzon, Ledesma, and others, in the Columbus lawsuit. Peter Martyr, however, collected his information on the subject independently. Varnhagen suggests that these navigators did not undertake their voyage, in 1508, after the return of Columbus, but in 1497, and that this was the first voyage of Vespucci.

The arguments for this alteration of eleven years in the date of a voyage of discovery are slight indeed. Oviedo, in his History of the Indies, wrote that the pilots Pinzon, Solis, and Ledesma discovered the Honduras coast with three vessels, before Pinzon was off the mouth of the Amazon, which was in 1499; and Gomara has the following passage: "but some say that Pinzon and Solis had been on the Honduras coast three years before Columbus." These writers were unscrupulous, and hostile to Columbus. It requires somewhat bold assurance to give the date of 1497 to the Pinzon and Solis voyages on the strength of these passages. Oviedo indeed puts Vespucci out of court at once, for he says that Pinzon, Solis, and Ledesma sailed with three vessels; while Vespucci asserts that in his first voyage there were four vessels. Moreover, Ledesma, who was pilot and captain of one of the vessels, was a lad of 21 in 1497, and could not have been in such a position; but in 1508, when the Pinzon and Solis expedition really sailed, he was of a suitable age. 44

Although the expedition of Pinzon, Solis, and Ledesma certainly did not take place in 1497, there has always been some obscurity attending its history, which has only recently been cleared up through the able researches of Mr. Harrisse. 45 The confusion has arisen from discrepancies between the evidence given by Pinzon and Ledesma in the Columbus lawsuit. Pinzon said that he reached the island of Guanaja in the Gulf of Honduras, and then followed the coast east as far as the provinces of Chabaca and Pintigron, and the mountains of Caria (Paria?). But Ledesma said that they went north from the island of Guanaja, came to Chabaca and Pintigron, and reached a point as far north as 23½°. Here there is clearly a mistake, one going east and the other north, yet both coming to Chabaca and Pintigron. It can only be decided whether the mistake is in the evidence of Pinzon or of Ledesma by ascertaining the positions of Chabaca and Pintigron; and the explanation is afforded by Peter Martyr in his second Decade. 46 He there says that Pinzon turned his course to the east ("towards the left hand") towards Paria, where princes came to him named Chiauaccha 47 and Pintiguanus. Ledesma's northerly course was either a falsehood, as Mr. Harrisse rather hastily assumes, or a clerical or printer's error. The only voyage of Pinzon and Solis took place in 1508, 48 and was from the Gulf of Honduras eastward to Paria.

There was no voyage of discovery sent by the King in 1497. When Diego Columbus instituted the lawsuit to recover his father's rights, the Crown lawyers turned every stone for evidence that others made discoveries besides the Admiral. The lawsuit lasted from 1508 to 1527. If an expedition sent by the King in 1497 had discovered 870 leagues of new coast-line, it is incredible that the proofs would not then have been forthcoming, when many of those who took part in the expedition must have been alive, and there was not only no reason for secrecy, but the strongest motive for publicity.

When the evidence respecting Pinzon and Solis was taken in 1516, Vespucci had been dead some years. He had never ventured to publish his letter in Spain; but Fernando Columbus purchased a copy at Rome and added it to his library at Seville in 1515, three years after Vespucci's death. If the first voyage had not been known to be a fabrication, the letter would have been eagerly brought forward as evidence of extensive discoveries not made by the Admiral. For by that time other copies, besides the one in Fernando's library, had probably reached Spain.

Then there is the negative evidence of maps. Juan de la Cosa drew his famous map of the world in 1500, after serving in the voyage of Hojeda, in company with Vespucci. He placed flags on the discovered parts, and one on each of the farthest known points. There is a Spanish flag at Cabo de la Vela, the extreme point then known in South America, another at the extreme point reached by Columbus on the north coast of Cuba, and an English flag at the extreme point reached by Cabot. A conjectural line runs round from the last English to the first Spanish flag, and there is no sign of the alleged Vespucci discoveries. If it is suggested that the Florentine himself kept them secret, without any conceivable object for doing so, there were all his companions to proclaim them, and there must have been an official report. If those 870 leagues of coast had been discovered, the discovery must have been shown on the map of Juan de la Cosa.

The Cantino map furnishes additional evidence against Vespucci of an interesting kind. This map of the world was compiled for the Duke of Ferrara by order of Alberto Cantino, to illustrate the voyages of Corte Real. It was drawn by a Portuguese draughtsman at Lisbon, and was finished in the autumn of 1502, having been paid for in November of that year. On the Cantino map, the coast-line discovered by Hojeda in 1499 is shown. It is not copied from the map of Juan de la Cosa, for most of the names are different 49; but the information must have been supplied by some one who was in Hojeda's expedition. Vespucci was in Lisbon in the autumn of 1502; it is, therefore, almost certain that this coast-line was laid down from information supplied by Vespucci. 50 If Vespucci, in 1497, had discovered a coast-line between 16° and 23° N., and another coast-line extending from 23° N. for 870 leagues N. W., these marvellous discoveries would also appear on the Cantino map. But there is not a sign of them. We may conclude from this that Vespucci had not yet conceived the idea of the fictitious voyage of 1497, when he assisted Cantino's draughtsman in the autumn of 1502. The imposture is first hinted at some six months afterwards in the Medici letter of March 1503. Peter Martyr gives corroborative evidence that Vespucci assisted the Portuguese cartographer. He says that he visited Bishop Fonseca, and was shown "many of those mappes which are commonly called the shipman cardes, or cardes of the sea: of the which, one was drawen by the Portugales, wherunto Americus Vesputius is said to have put his hande, beinge a man experte in this facultie, and a Florentine borne." 51

Further evidence against Vespucci is furnished by the map which was prepared in 1511 to illustrate Peter Martyr's Decades. This author was personally acquainted with Vespucci, who was then chief pilot of Spain, and was intimate with his nephew Giovanni. Yet there is not a sign of Vespucci's alleged discoveries in 1497 on the map of 1511. There was no motive for secrecy on the part of Vespucci, or on the part of the captains and pilots of the four ships; on the contrary, their interest was to make the discoveries public and get credit for them. Bermuda appears for the first time on the map of 1511, having been discovered by Juan Bermudez. But there is no mention of Iti. In this same year, Ponce de Leon obtained a concession for the discovery of that very coast of Florida which, according to Varnhagen, had been discovered in its whole extent by Vespucci fourteen years before. The concession was actually made on the condition that the coast had not been discovered before, and Vespucci was then chief pilot. It is incredible that Vespucci and all his companions should have combined to conceal their wonderful discoveries without any conceivable reason, their silence being most injurious to themselves. It is still more incredible that the King should have put such a condition into the concession to Ponce de Leon, if it was true that the coast in question had been discovered fourteen years before by an expedition despatched by himself.

The evidence against Vespucci is cumulative and quite conclusive. His first voyage is a fabrication. He cannot be acquitted of the intention of appropriating for himself the glory of having first discovered the mainland. The impartial and upright Las Casas, after carefully weighing the evidence, found him guilty. This verdict has been, and will continue to be, confirmed by posterity. He wished to glorify himself in his own country, whither he intended to retire, and throughout Europe. But he did not dare to publish his fiction in Spain, and, so far as we know, it did not reach Spain in print until after his death. He wrote well, and his stories about a new world excited the enthusiasm of those who read them. His Latin editor suggested that his new world should be called America, and the name was adopted by map-makers. It was euphonious and convenient, and, in spite of the protests of Las Casas and Herrera, it eventually became general, and Vespucci usurped the honours that rightly belonged to Columbus. Vespucci may be acquitted of having contemplated so great an injustice. It is possible that he never intended that his letters should be published. He may only have desired to increase his consequence among his own countrymen. But whatever his intention may have been, he committed a fraud with a dishonest purpose, and it is no extenuation that he did not contemplate the full extent of the injustice it has caused.

The investigation of Vespucci's statements contained in the first and second voyages destroys all confidence in his unsupported word, when we proceed to examine his account of the voyages alleged to have been made by him in Portuguese ships.

There is no mention either of Vespucci or of Giocondi, who is alleged to have brought him the invitation from the King to come to Portugal, either in the voluminous Portuguese archives, or in the contemporary chronicle of Damian de Goes. This remarkable silence points to the conclusion that if Vespucci was really in any Portuguese expedition he can only have filled some very subordinate post; probably sailing as a merchant or a volunteer. 52

Vespucci has given us two accounts of his alleged first voyage with the Portuguese, which he calls his third voyage. The Medici letter is entirely devoted to it, while it is also included in the Soderini letter. The dates and figures seldom agree in the two letters, and there is evidence throughout them of the random way in which he wrote, and of his disregard for truth or accuracy. Sailing with three vessels, on the 10th of March 1501 according to one letter, and on the 15th according to the other, they came to a place called Bezeguiche, or Beseghir, 53 on the west coast of Africa, which Vespucci identifies as Cape Verd, and places in 14° 30′ N. in one letter, and in 13° within the Tropic in the other. 54 Thence they sailed across the ocean for sixty-seven days, or sixty-three days, on a S.W. ¼ S. course for 700 leagues, reaching the coast on the 7th or 17th of August, in 5° S. latitude. In the Soderini letter there is a story of Portuguese being murdered and eaten; but in the Medici letter there is nothing but friendly intercourse with the natives, with a long account of their manners and customs, obviously as fictitious as those in the first voyage which were commented upon by Las Casas. Among the plants he saw, Vespucci gives the names of four: cannafistula, Brazil wood, cassia, and myrrh.

From the landfall they sailed eastward for (150) 300 leagues, to a point of land which was named Cape St. Augustine, and then south and west as far as 52° S. Vespucci alleges that the command of the fleet was given to him, and that he continued a southerly course. In the Medici letter he says that he went south until he was 17° 30′ from the Antarctic Pole, or in 73° 30′ S., which is preposterous. In the Soderini letter he reached only 52° S., got into a gale of wind, sighted some land with a rocky coast, and ran along it for 20 leagues. 55 Thence the ships shaped a homeward course, reached Sierra Leone on June 10th—where one vessel was condemned as unseaworthy, and burnt—the Azores in the end of July, and Lisbon on September 7th, 1502. Both letters contain some absurd remarks about the stars in the southern hemisphere, and one has a long explanation how two men, one in 39° N. and another in 50° S., would be standing at right angles to each other.

The second voyage of Vespucci from Lisbon; which he calls his fourth voyage, was undertaken for the discovery of Malacca, which he believed to be in 33° S. latitude, instead of 2° 14′ N. latitude, its real position. This is a pretty considerable error! The narrative is full of spiteful and vindictive remarks about the commander of the expedition, whose name is not given. 56 One vessel was lost off an island which appears to have been Fernando Noronha, and two others, with Vespucci, reached the coast of Brazil and entered a harbour, which was named Bahia do todos os Santos. They then sailed along the coast for 260 leagues, where they found another harbour in 18° S. Here they built a fort, and, leaving a garrison, returned to Lisbon on June 18th, 1504.

The two Portuguese voyages may be authentic, though the absence of all names, and the silence of the Lisbon archives touching Vespucci, make it impossible to identify them. The careless and unreliable way in which Vespucci tells his story renders it worse than useless to speculate on any of the details, beyond the fact that the Portuguese commanders appear to have explored a considerable part of the coast of Brazil. Any theory based on the latitudes given by Vespucci would only mislead, for, when the places to which they refer can be identified, they are wrong, and when given in both the letters, they differ. The letter describing the four voyages was not written for readers acquainted with the history and progress of discovery, not for Spaniards or Portuguese, but for the Medicis and Soderinis, the Waldseemüllers and Ringmanns, to whom these tales were new, wonderful, and mysterious. Accuracy and truth were of no consequence so long as they believed in Amerigo Vespucci as the discoverer of the New World and its marvels.

The tales of Amerigo Vespucci have a place in the history of geographical discovery, and require, although they do not deserve, serious consideration; the more so as they have, in recent years, been treated seriously by a learned and accomplished writer such as Varnhagen, who has been followed by one or two eminent and well-known men of letters. It is, therefore, proper that translations of the letters should be printed by the Hakluyt Society, and that their merits should be fully discussed.

In addition to the two letters of Vespucci, the present volume contains the evidence taken in the Columbus lawsuit bearing on the subject, the chapters in the history of Las Casas in which the veracity of Vespucci is discussed, the narrative of the voyage of Hojeda from Navarrete, and some other documents throwing light on the career of the Florentine adventurer.

Letter of Amerigo Vespucci

On the Islands Newly Discovered in His Four Voyages.

First Voyage of Amerigo Vespucci.

57

Magnificent Lord. 58 I submit humble reverence to you and offer due recommendations. It may be that your Magnificence will be astonished at my temerity that I should dare so absurdly to write the present long letter to your Magnificence, knowing that your Magnificence is constantly occupied in the high councils and affairs touching the lofty Republic. And I may be considered not only presumptuous but also idle in writing things not convenient to your condition nor agreeable, and written in a barbarous style. But as I have confidence in your virtues and in the merit of my writing, which is touching things never before written upon either by ancient or modern writers, as will be seen, I may be excused by your Magnificence. The principal thing that moved me to write to you was the request of the bearer, who is named Benvenuto Benvenuti, our Florentine, who is very much the servant of your Magnificence, as he tells me, and a great friend of mine. He, finding himself here in this city of Lisbon, requested me to give an account to your Magnificence of the things by me seen in different parts of the world, during the four voyages that I have made to discover new lands; two by order of the Catholic King Ferdinand, by the Great Gulf of the Ocean Sea towards the west, the other two by order of the powerful King Manoel of Portugal, towards the south. He assured me that you will be pleased, and that in this I might hope to serve you. It was this that disposed me to do it, being assured that your Magnificence would include me in the number of your servants, remembering how, in the time of our youth, I was your friend, and now your servant, going together to hear the principles of grammar under the good life and doctrine of the venerable religious friar of St. Mark, Friar Giorgio Antonio Vespucci, whose counsels and doctrine, if it had pleased God that I had followed, I should have been another man from what I am, as Petrarch says. Quomodocunque sit, I am not ashamed, because I have always taken delight in virtuous things. Yet if these my frivolities are not acceptable to your virtue, I will reflect on what Pliny said to Mæcenas, "Formerly my witticisms used to entertain you." It may be that, though your Magnificence is continually occupied with public affairs, you may find an hour of leisure, during which you can pass a little time in frivolous or amusing things, and so, as a change from so many occupations, you may read this my letter. For you may well turn for a brief space from constant care and assiduous thought concerning public affairs.

Your Magnificence must know that the motive of my coming into this kingdom of Spain was to engage in mercantile pursuits, and that I was occupied in such business for nearly four years, during which I saw and knew various changes of fortune. As these affairs of commerce are uncertain, a man being at one time at the top of the well, and at another fallen and subject to losses, and as the continual labour that a man is exposed to who would succeed, became evident to me, as well as exposure to dangers and failures, I decided upon leaving the mercantile career, and upon entering on one that would be more stable and praiseworthy. I was disposed to see some part of the world and its wonders.

Time and opportunity offered themselves very conveniently. The King Don Fernando of Castille, 59 having ordered four ships to be dispatched for the discovery of new lands towards the west, I was chosen by his Highness to go in this fleet to help in the discovery. I left the port of Cadiz on the 10th of May 60 1497, and we took our way for the Great Gulf of the Ocean Sea, on which voyage I was engaged for eighteen months, discovering a great extent of mainland, and an infinite number of islands, most of them inhabited, of which no mention had been made by ancient writers, I believe because they had not any clear information. If I remember rightly, I have read somewhere that this Ocean Sea was without inhabitants. Our poet Dante was of this opinion, in the 26th chapter of the Inferno, where he treats of the death of Ulysses. 61 In this voyage I saw many wonderful things, as your Magnificence will understand. As I said before, we left the port of Cadiz in four ships, and began our navigation to the Fortunate Islands, which are now called the Grand Canaria, situated in the Ocean Sea, on the confines of the inhabited west, within the third climate. 62 Over which place the Pole rises from the north, above the horizon 27° and a half, and it is distant from this city of Lisbon 280 leagues, 63 between south and south-west. Here we staid for eight days, providing ourselves with wood, water, and other necessaries. From thence, having offered our prayers, we weighed, and spread our sails to the wind, shaping our course to the west, with a point to south-west. 64 Our progress was such that at the end of thirty-seven days 65 we reached land which we judged to be the mainland, being distant from the island of Canaria, more to the west, nearly 1,000 leagues, 66 outside that which is inhabited in the Torrid Zone. For we found the North Pole was above its horizon 16°; and more to the westward than the island of Canaria, according to the observations with our instruments 70°. 67

We anchored with our ships at a distance of a league and a half from the shore. We got out the boats, and, filled with armed men, we pulled them to the shore. Before we arrived we had seen many men walking along the beach, at which we were much pleased; and we found that they were naked, and they showed fear of us, I believe because we were dressed and of a different stature. They all fled to a hill, and, in spite of all the signs of peace and friendship that we made, they would not come to have intercourse with us. As night was coming on, and the ship was anchored in a dangerous place, off an open unsheltered coast, we arranged to get under weigh the next day, and to go in search of some port or bay where we could make our ships secure. We sailed along the coast to the north, always in sight of land, and the people went along the beach. After two days of navigation we found a very secure place for the ships, and we anchored at a distance of half a league from the land, where we saw very many people. We went on shore in the boats on the same day, and forty men in good order landed. The natives were still shy of us, and we could not give them sufficient confidence to induce them to come and speak with us. That day we worked so hard with this object by giving them our things, such as bells, looking-glasses, and other trifles, that some of them took courage and came to treat with us. Having established a friendly understanding, as the night was approaching we took leave of them, and returned on board. Next day, at dawn, we saw that there were an immense number of people on the beach, and that they had their women and children with them. We went on shore, and found that they all came laden with their food supplies, which are such as will be described in their place. Before we arrived on shore, many of them swam out to receive us at a cross-bow shot's distance; for they are great swimmers, and they showed as much confidence as if we had been having intercourse with them for a long time; and we were pleased at seeing their feelings of security.

What we knew of their life and customs was that they all go naked, as well the men as the women, without covering anything, no otherwise than as they come out of their mothers' wombs. They are of medium stature, and very well proportioned. The colour of their skins inclines to red, like the skin of a lion, and I believe that, if they were properly clothed, they would be white like ourselves. They have no hair whatever on their bodies, but they have very long black hair, especially the women, which beautifies them. They have not very beautiful faces, because they have long eyelids, which make them look like Tartars. They do not allow any hairs to grow on their eyebrows, nor eyelashes, nor in any other part except on the head, where it is rough and dishevelled. They are very agile in their persons, both in walking and running, as well the men as the women; and think nothing of running a league or two, as we often witnessed; and in this they have a very great advantage over us Christians. They swim wonderfully well, and the women better than the men; for we have found and seen them many times two leagues at sea, without any help whatever in swimming.

Their arms are bows and arrows, well made, except that they have no iron, nor any other kind of hard metal. Instead of iron they use teeth of animals or of fish, or a bit of wood well burnt at the point. They are sure shots, and where they aim they hit. In some places the women use these bows. They have other weapons like lances, hardened by fire, and clubs with the knobs very well carved. They wage war among themselves with people who do not speak their language, carrying it on with great cruelty, giving no quarter, if not inflicting greater punishment. When they go to war they take their women with them; not because they fight, but because they carry the provisions in rear of the men. A woman carries a burden on her back, which a man would not carry, for thirty or forty leagues, as we have seen many times. They have no leader, nor do they march in any order, no one being captain. The cause of their wars is not the desire of rule nor to extend the limits of their dominions, but owing to some ancient feud that has arisen among them in former times. When asked why they made war, they have no other answer than that it is to avenge the death of their ancestors and their fathers. They have neither king nor lord, nor do they obey anyone, but live in freedom. Having moved themselves to wage war, when the enemy have killed or captured any of them, the oldest relation arises and goes preaching through the streets and calling upon his countrymen to come with him to avenge the death of his relation, and thus he moves them by compassion. They do not bring men to justice, nor punish a criminal. Neither the mother nor the father chastise their children, and it is wonderful that we never saw a quarrel among them. They show themselves simple in their talk, and are very sharp and cunning in securing their ends. They speak little, and in a low voice. They use the same accents as ourselves, forming their words either on the palate, the teeth, or the lips, only they have other words for things. Great is the diversity of languages, for in a hundred leagues we found such change in the language that the inhabitants could not understand each other.

Their mode of life is very barbarous, for they have no regular time for their meals, but they eat at any time that they have the wish, as often at night as in the day—indeed, they eat at all hours. They take their food on the ground, without napkin or any other cloth, eating out of earthen pots which they make, or out of half calabashes. They sleep in certain very large nets made of cotton, 69 and suspended in the air; and if this should seem a bad way of sleeping, I say that it is pleasant to sleep in that manner, and that we slept better in that way than in coverlets. 70 They are a people of cleanly habits as regards their bodies, and are constantly washing themselves. When they empty the stomach they do everything so as not to be seen, and in this they are clean and decent; but in making water they are dirty and without shame, for while talking with us they do such things without turning round, and without any shame. They do not practise matrimony among them, each man taking as many women as he likes, and when he is tired of a woman he repudiates her without either injury to himself or shame to the woman, for in this matter the woman has the same liberty as the man. They are not very jealous, but lascivious beyond measure, the women much more so than the men. I do not further refer to their contrivances for satisfying their inordinate desires, so that I may not offend against modesty. They are very prolific in bearing children, and in their pregnancy they are not excused any work whatever. The parturition is so easy, and accompanied by so little pain, that they are up and about the next day. They go to some river to wash, and presently are quite well, appearing on the water like fish. If they are angry with their husbands they easily cause abortion with certain poisonous herbs or roots, and destroy the child. Many infants perish in this way. They are gifted with very handsome and well-proportioned bodies, and no part or member is to be seen that is not well formed. Although they go naked, yet that which should be concealed is kept between the thighs so that it cannot be seen. Yet there no one cares, for the same impression is made on them at seeing anything indecent as is made on us at seeing a nose or mouth. Among them it is considered strange if a woman has wrinkles on the bosom from frequent parturition, or on the belly. All parts are invariably preserved after the parturition as they were before. They showed an excessive desire for our company.

We did not find that these people had any laws; they cannot be called Moors nor Jews, but worse than Gentiles. For we did not see that they offered any sacrifices, nor have they any place of worship. I judge their lives to be Epicurean. Their habitations are in common. Their dwellings, are like huts, but strongly built of very large trees, and covered with palm leaves, secure from tempests and winds. In some places they are of such length and width that we found 600 souls in one single house. We found villages of only thirteen houses where there were 4,000 inhabitants. They build the villages every eight or ten years, and when asked why they did this, they replied that it was because the soil was corrupted and infected, and caused diseases in their bodies, so they chose a new site. Their wealth consists of the feathers of birds of many colours, or "paternosters" made of the fins of fishes, or of white or green stones, which they wear on their necks, lips, and ears; and of many other things which have no value for us. They have no commerce, and neither buy nor sell. In conclusion, they live, and are content with what nature has given them.

They have none of the riches which are looked upon as such in our Europe and in other parts, such as gold, pearls, or precious stones: and even if they have them in their country, they do not work to get them. They are liberal in their giving, for it is wonderful if they refuse anything, and also liberal in asking, as soon as they make friends. Their greatest sign of friendship is to give their wives or daughters, and a father and mother considered themselves highly honoured when they brought us a daughter, especially if she was a virgin, that we should sleep with her, and in doing this they use terms of warm friendship.

When they die they use several kinds of burial. Some bury their dead with water and food, thinking they will want it. They have no ceremonies of lights, nor of weeping. In some other places they practise a most barbarous and inhuman kind of interment. This is that when a sick or infirm person is almost in the throes of death, his relations carry him into a great wood, and fasten one of those nets in which they sleep to two trees. They put their dying relation into it, and dance round him the whole of one day. When night comes on they put water and food enough for four or six days at his head, and then leave him alone, returning to their village. If the sick man can help himself, and eats and lives so as to return to the village, they receive him with ceremony, but few are those who escape. Most of them die, and that is their sepulchre. They have many other customs, which are omitted to avoid prolixity. In their illnesses they use various kinds of medicines, so different from ours that we marvelled how anyone escaped. I often saw a patient ill with fever, when the disease was at its height; bathed with quantities of cold water from head to foot. Then they made a great fire all round, making him turn backwards and forwards for two hours until he was tired, and he was then left to sleep. Many were cured. They also attend to the diet, keep the patient without food, and draw blood, not from the arm, but from the thighs and loins, and from the calves of the legs. They also provoke vomiting by putting one of their herbs into the mouth, and they use many other remedies which it would take long to recount. They abound much in phlegm and in blood, on account of their food, which consists of roots, fruit, and fish. They have no sowing of grain, nor of any kind of corn. But for their common use they eat the root of a tree, from which they make very good flour, and they call it Iuca. 71 Others call it Cazabi 72 and Ignami. 73 They eat little flesh, unless it be human flesh, and your Magnificence must know that they are so inhuman as to transgress regarding this most bestial custom. For they eat all their enemies that they kill or take, as well females as males, with so much barbarity that it is a brutal thing to mention, how much more to see it, as has happened to me an infinite number of times. They were astonished at us when we told them that we did not eat our enemies. Your Magnificence may believe for certain that they have many other barbarous customs, for in these four voyages I have seen so many things different from our customs that I have written a book, 74 to be called The Four Voyages, in which I have related the greater part of the things I saw, very clearly and to the best of my abilities. I have not yet published it, because my own affairs are in such a bad state that I have no taste for what I have written, yet I am much inclined to publish it. In this work will be seen all the events in detail, I therefore do not enlarge upon them here. For in the course of the said work we shall see many other special details; so this will suffice for what is general. In this beginning I did not see anything of much value in the land except some indications of gold. I believe that this was because we did not know the language, and so we could not benefit by the resources of the land.

We resolved to depart and to proceed onwards, coasting along the land; in which voyage we made many tacks, and had intercourse with many tribes. At the end of certain days we came to a port where we were in the greatest danger, and it pleased the Lord to save us. It was in this way. We went on shore in a port where we found a village built over a lake, like Venice. There were about forty-four large houses founded on very thick piles, and each had a drawbridge leading to the door. From one house there was a way to all the rest by drawbridges which led from house to house. The people of this little city showed signs that they were afraid of us, and suddenly they rose all at once. While looking at this wonder, we saw about twenty-two canoes coming over the sea, which are the sort of boats they use, hollowed out of a single tree. They came to our ships, as if to gaze with wonder at us and our clothes, but they kept at a distance. Things being so, we made signs to them to come to us, giving them assurances of friendship. Seeing that they did not come we went to them, but they did not wait for us. They went on shore, and made signs to us that we should wait, and that they would soon return. They went straight to a hill, and were not long before they came back, leading with them sixteen of their young girls. They got into the canoes and came to the ships, and in each ship they put four, and we were as much surprised at such a proceeding as your Magnificence will be. They were amongst our ships with the canoes, speaking with us. We looked upon this as a sign of friendship. Presently a number of people came swimming over the sea, and approached us without our feeling any suspicion whatever, having come from the houses. Then certain old women appeared at the doors of the houses, uttering great cries and tearing their hair in sign of grief. This made us suspect something, and each man seized his arms. Suddenly the young girls who were on board jumped into the sea, and those in the canoes came nearer, and began to shoot with their bows and arrows. Those who were swimming had each brought a lance, concealed under the water as much as possible. As soon as we understood the treachery we not only defended ourselves from them, but also attacked them vigorously and sank many of their canoes with our ships. Thus we routed and slaughtered them, and all took to swimming, abandoning their canoes. Having thus suffered enough damage, they swam to the land. Nearly fifteen or twenty of them were killed, and many were wounded. Of our men five were wounded, and all escaped, thanks to God. We captured two girls and two men. We went to their houses and entered them, but only found two old women and one sick man. We took many of their things, but they were of little value. We would not burn their houses, because we felt compunctions of conscience. We returned to our ships with five prisoners, and put irons on the feet of each, except the girls. On the following night the two girls and one of the men escaped with great cunning. Next day we decided upon continuing our course onwards.

We sailed constantly along the coast, and came to another tribe, distant about 80 leagues from the one we had left, and very different both as regards language and customs. We came to an anchor, and went on shore in the boats, when we saw that a great number of people were on the beach, upwards of 4,000 souls. They did not wait for our landing, but took to flight, abandoning their things. We jumped on shore, and went along a road which led to the woods. At the distance of a cross-bow shot we found their huts, where they had made very large fires, and two were there cooking their food, and roasting animals and fish of many sorts. Here we saw that they were roasting a certain animal like a serpent, except that it had no wings, and its appearance was so horrid that many of us wondered at its fierceness. We walked to their houses or sheds, and they had many of these serpents alive, fastened by their feet and with a cord round the snout, so that they could not open their mouths, as is done to pointers, 75 to prevent them from biting. Their aspect was so fierce that none of us dared to go near one, thinking they were poisonous. They are the size of a young goat, and a fathom and a half long. They have long and thick feet, armed with large claws, the skin hard and of various colours. The mouth and face are like those of a serpent. They have a crest like a saw, which extends from the nose to the end of the tail. We concluded that they were serpents and poisonous, yet they eat them. 76 We found that the natives made bread of small fishes, which they take from the sea, first boiling them, then pounding them into a paste, and roasting them in the cinders, and so they are eaten. We tried them, and found them good. They have so many other kinds of food, and a greater number of fruits and roots, that it would take long to describe them in detail. Seeing that the people did not come back, we determined not to touch any of their things, to give them more confidence. We also left many of our own things in their huts, that they might see them, and at night we returned to the ships. Next day, at dawn, we saw an immense crowd of people on the beach, so we went on shore. When they again showed fear we reassured them, and induced them to treat with us, giving them everything they asked for. When they became friendly they told us that those were their habitations, and that they were come to fish. They asked us to come to their villages that they might receive us as friends. They showed such friendship because of the two men we had prisoners, who were their enemies. Seeing their importunity, and after a consultation, we decided that twenty-eight of our Christians, in good order, should go with them, with the firm intention to die if it should be necessary. When we had been there nearly three days we went with them into the interior. At a distance of three leagues from the beach we came to a village of few houses and many inhabitants, there not being more than nine habitations. Here we were received with so many barbarous ceremonies that the pen will not suffice to write them down. There were songs, dances, tears mingled with rejoicings, and plenty of food. We remained here for the night. Here they offered their wives to us, and we were unable to defend ourselves from them. We remained all night and half the next day. The multitude of people who came to see us was such that they could not be counted. The older men prayed that we would come with them to another village further in the interior, making signs that they would show us the greatest honour. So we agreed to go, and it cannot be expressed what great honour they showed us. We came to many villages, and were nine days on the journey, so that our Christians who remained on board became anxious about us. Being nearly eighteen leagues inland in a direct line, we determined to return to the ships. On the return journey the crowd was so great that came with us to the beach, both of women and men, that it was wonderful. If any of our people got tired on the way, they carried them in their nets very comfortably. In crossing the rivers, which are numerous and very large, they took us across by their contrivances so safely that there was no danger whatever. Many of them came laden with the things they had given to us, which were their sleeping-nets, most of them richly worked, numerous parrots of various colours, many bows and arrows; while others carried burdens consisting of their provisions and animals. What greater wonder can I tell you than that they thought themselves fortunate when, in passing a river, they could carry us on their backs?

Having reached the shore, we went on board the ships. They made such a crowd to enter our ships in order to see them, that we were astonished. We took as many as we could in the boats, and took them to the ships, and so many came swimming that we were inclined to stop such a crowd from being on board, more than a thousand souls, all naked and without arms. They wondered at our arrangements and contrivances, and at the size of the ships. There happened a laughable thing, which was that we had occasion to fire off some of our artillery, and when the report was heard, the greater part of the natives on board jumped overboard from fear, and began to swim, like the frogs on the banks, which, when they are frightened, jump into the swamp. Such was the conduct of these people. Those who remained on board were so frightened that we were sorry we had done it, but we reassured them by saying that we frightened our enemies with those arms. Having amused themselves all day on board, we told them that they must go, because we wished to depart that night; and so they went away with much show of love and friendship, returning to the shore. Among this tribe, and in their land, I knew and saw so much of their customs and mode of life that I do not care to enlarge upon them here; for your Magnificence must know that in each of my voyages I have noted down the most remarkable things, and all is reduced into a volume in the geographical style, entitled the Four Voyages, in which work all things are described in detail, but I have not yet sent out a copy, because it is necessary for me to revise it.

This land is very populous and full of people, with numerous rivers, but few animals. They are similar to ours, except the lions, ounces, stags, pigs, goats, and deer; and these still have some differences of form. They have neither horses nor mules, asses nor dogs, nor any kind of sheep, nor cattle. But they have many other animals all wild, and none of them serve for any domestic use, so that they cannot be counted. What shall we say of the birds, which are so many, and of so many kinds and colours of plumage that it is wonderful to see them? The land is very pleasant and fruitful, full of very large woods and forests, and it is always green, for the trees never shed their leaves. The fruits are so numerous that they cannot be enumerated, and all different from ours. This land is within the Torrid Zone, under the parallel which the Tropic of Cancer describes, where the Pole is 23° above the horizon, on the verge of the second climate. Many people came to see us, and were astonished at our appearance and the whiteness of our skins. They asked whence we came, and we gave them to understand that we came from heaven, and that we were travelling to see the world, and they believed it. In this land we put up a font of baptism, and an infinite number of people were baptised, and they called us, in their language, Carabi, which is as much as to say, "men of great wisdom."

We departed from this port. The province is called Parias, 77 and we navigated along the coast, always in sight of land, until we had run along it a distance of 870 leagues, always towards the North-West, 78 making many tacks and treating with many tribes. In many places we discovered gold, though not in any great quantity, but we did much in discovering the land, and in ascertaining that there was gold. We had now been thirteen months on the voyage, 79 and the ships and gear were much worn, and the men tired. We resolved, after consultation, to beach the ships and heave them down, as they were making much water, and to caulk them afresh, before shaping a course for Spain. When we made this decision we were near the finest harbour in the world, which we entered with our ships. Here we found a great many people, who received us in a very friendly manner. On shore we made a bastion with our boats, and with casks and our guns, at which we all rejoiced. Here we lightened 80 and cleared our ships, and hauled them up, making all the repairs that were necessary, the people of the country giving us all manner of help, and regularly supplying us with provisions. For in that port we had little relish for our own, which we made fun of, for our provisions for the voyage were running short, and were bad.

We remained here thirty-seven days, and often went to their village, where they received us with great honour. When we wanted to resume our voyage, they made a complaint how, at certain times, a very cruel and hostile tribe came by way of the sea to their land, murdered many of them, subdued them, and took some prisoners, carrying them off to their own houses and land. They added that they were scarcely able to defend themselves, making signs that their enemies were people of an island at a distance of about 100 leagues out at sea. They said this so earnestly that we believed them; and we promised to avenge their injuries, which gave them much pleasure. Many of them offered to go with us, but we did not wish to take them. We agreed that seven should accompany us, on condition that they went in their own canoe. For we did not want to be obliged to take them back to their land; and they were content. So we took leave of those people, leaving many friends among them.

Our ships having been repaired, we navigated for seven days across the sea, with the wind 81 between north-east and east, and at the end of the seven days we came upon the islands, which were numerous, some inhabited and others deserted. We anchored off one of them, where we saw many people, who called it Iti. 82 Having manned our boats with good men, and placed three rounds of the bombard in each, we pulled to the shore, where we found 400 men and many women, all naked. They were well made, and seemed good fighting men, for they were armed with bows and arrows, and lances. The greater part of them also had square shields, and they carried them so that they should not impede their using the bow. As we approached the shore in the boats, at the distance of a bowshot, they all rushed into the water to shoot their arrows, and to defend themselves from us they returned to the land. They all had their bodies painted with different colours, and were adorned with feathers. The interpreters told us that when they showed themselves plumed and painted, it is a sign that they intend to fight. They so persevered in defending the landing that we were obliged to use our artillery. When they heard the report, and saw some of their own people fall dead, they all retreated inland. After holding a consultation, we resolved to land forty of our men, and await their attack. The men landed with their arms, and the natives came against us, and fought us for nearly an hour, 83 gaining little advantage, except that our cross-bow men and gunners killed some of the natives, while they wounded some of our people. They would not wait for the thrust of our spears or swords, but we pushed on with such vigour at last that we came within sword-thrust, and as they could not withstand our arms, they fled to the hills and woods, leaving us victorious on the field, with many of their dead and wounded. We did not continue the pursuit that day, because we were very tired. In returning to the ships, the seven men who came with us showed such delight that they could not contain themselves.

Next day we saw a great number of the people on shore, still with signs of war, sounding horns and various other instruments used by them for defiance, and all plumed and painted, so that it was a very strange thing to behold them. All the ships, therefore, consulted together, and it was concluded that these people desired hostility with us. It was then decided that we should do all in our power to make friends with them, and if they rejected our friendship we should treat them as enemies, and that we should make slaves of as many as we could take. Being armed as well as our means admitted, we returned to the shore. They did not oppose our landing, I believe from fear of the guns. Forty of our men landed in four detachments, each with a captain, and attacked them. After a long battle, many of them being killed, the rest were put to flight. We followed in pursuit until we came to a village, having taken nearly 250 prisoners. 84 We burnt the village and returned to the ships with these 250 prisoners, leaving many killed and wounded. On our side no more than one was killed, and twenty-two were wounded, who all recovered. God be thanked! We prepared to depart, and the seven men, five of whom were wounded, took a canoe belonging to the island, and with seven prisoners that we gave them, four women and three men, they returned to their land with much joy, astonished at our power. We made sail for Spain with 222 prisoners, 85 our slaves, and arrived in the port of Cadiz on the 15th of October 1498, where we were well received, and where we sold our slaves. This is what befell me in this my first voyage, that was most worthy of note.

THE FIRST VOYAGE ENDS.

Second Voyage of Amerigo Vespucci.

As regards the second voyage, what I saw in it most worthy of mention is as follows: We left the port of Cadiz, with three ships, 86 on the 16th of May 1499, and shaped our course direct for the Cape Verde islands, passing in sight of the island of Grand Canary; and we navigated until we reached an island which is called the island of Fuoco. Here we got in our supplies of wood and water, and thence shaped our course to the south-west. In forty-four days we came in sight of a new land, and we judged it to be the mainland, continuous with that of which mention has already been made. This land is within the Torrid Zone, and beyond the equinoctial line on the south side, over which the Pole rises from the meridian 5°, beyond every climate. It is distant from the said islands by the S.W. wind 87 500 leagues. We found the day and night to be equal, because we arrived on the 27th of June, when the sun is near the tropic of Cancer. We found this land to be all drowned, and full of very great rivers. At first we did not see any people. We anchored our ships and got our boats out, going with them to the land, which, as I have said, we found to be full of very large rivers, and drowned by these great rivers. There we tried in many directions to see if we could enter; and owing to the great waters and rivers, in spite of so much labour, we could not find a place that was not inundated.

We saw, along the rivers, many signs of the country being inhabited; but having ascertained that we could not enter from this part, we determined to return to the ships, and to try another part. We weighed our anchors, and navigated between the east south-east, coasting along the land, which trended southwards, and many times we made forty leagues, but all was time lost. We found on this coast that the current of the sea had such force that it prevented us from navigating, for it ran from south to north. The inconvenience was so great for our navigation that, after a consultation, we decided upon altering the course to north, and we made good such a distance along the land, that we reached a most excellent port, formed by a large island, which was at the entrance. 88 Within, a very large haven was formed.

In sailing along the island to enter it we saw many people, and we steered our ships so as to bring them up where the people were seen, which was nearly four leagues more towards the sea. Sailing in this way we had seen a canoe, which was coming from seaward, with many people on board. We de-

33

termined to overhaul her, and we went round with our ships in her direction, so that we might not lose her. Sailing towards the canoe with a fresh breeze, we saw that they had stopped with their oars tossed—I believe, with wonder at the sight of our ships. But when they saw that we were gaining upon them, they put down their oars, and began to row towards the land. As our company came in a fast-sailing caravel of forty-five tons, we got to windward of the canoe, and when it seemed time to bear down upon her, the sheets were eased off so as to come near her; and as the caravel seemed to be coming down upon her, and those on board did not wish to be caught, they pulled away to leeward, and, seeing their advantage, they gave way with their oars to escape. As we had our boats at the stern well manned, we thought we should catch the canoe. The boats chased for more than two hours, and at last the caravel made another tack, but could not fetch the canoe. As the people in the canoe saw they were closely pressed by the caravel and the boats, they all jumped into the sea, their number being about seventy men; the distance from the shore being nearly two leagues. Following them in the boats, during the whole day, we were unable to capture more than two, all the rest escaping on shore. Only four boys remained in the canoe, who were not of their tribe, but prisoners from some other land. They had been castrated, and were all without the virile member, and with the scars fresh, at which we wondered much. Having taken them on board, they told us by signs that they had been castrated to be eaten. We then knew that the people in the canoe belonged to a tribe called Cambali, very fierce men who eat human flesh. We came with the ship, towing the canoe astern, approaching the land, and anchored at a distance of half a league. We saw a great number of people on the beach, so we went on shore with the boats, taking with us the two men we had captured. When we came near all the people fled into the wood. So we released one of our prisoners, giving him many signs that we wanted to be their friends. He did what we wanted very well, and brought back all the people with him, numbering about 400 men and many women, and they came unarmed to the boats. A good understanding was established with them; we released the other prisoner, sent to the ships for their canoe, and restored it to them. This canoe was twenty-six paces long, and two braccia 89 in width, all dug out of a single tree, and very well worked. When they had hauled it up and put it in a secure place, they all fled, and would not have anything more to do with us; which seemed a barbarous act, and we judged them to be a faithless and ill-conditioned people. We saw a little gold, which they wear in their ears.

We departed and entered the bay, where we found so many people that it was wonderful. We made friends with them, and many of us went with them to their villages in great security. In this place we collected 150 pearls, which they gave us for a small bell, and a little gold was given to us for nothing. In this land we found that they drank wine made from their fruits and seeds, like beer, both white and red. The best was made from plums, 90 and it was very good. We ate a great many of them, as they were in season. It is a very good fruit, pleasant to the taste, and wholesome for the body. The land abounds in their articles of food, and the people are of good manners, and the most peaceful we have yet met with. We were seventeen days in this port, enjoying it very much, and every day new people from the interior came to see us, wondering at our faces and the whiteness of our skins, at our clothes and arms, and at the shape and size of our ships. From these people we had tidings that there was another tribe to the westward who were their enemies, and who had an immense quantity of pearls. Those which they possessed had been taken in their wars. They told us how they were fished, and in what manner the pearls were born, and we found their information to be correct, as your Magnificence will hear.

We left this port and sailed along the coast, always seeing people on the beach, and at the end of many days we came to in a port, by reason of the necessity for repairing one of our ships, which made much water. Here we found many people, but were unable, either by force or persuasion, to establish any intercourse with them. When we went on shore they opposed the landing fiercely, and when they could do no more they fled into the woods and did not wait for us. Seeing that they were such barbarians we departed thence, and, sailing onwards, we came in sight of an island which was fifteen leagues from the land. We decided upon going to see whether it was inhabited. We found on it the most bestial and the most brutal race that has ever been seen, and they were of this kind. They were very brutish in appearance and gesture, and they had their mouths full of the leaves of a green herb, which they continually chewed like beasts, so that they could hardly speak; and each had round his neck two dry gourds, one full of that herb which they had in their mouths, and the other of white flour that appeared to be powdered lime. From time to time they put in the powder with a spindle which they kept wet in the mouth. Then they put stuff into their mouths from both, powdering the herb already in use. They did this with much elaboration; and the thing seemed wonderful, for we could not understand the secret, or with what object they did it. 91

These people, when they saw us, came to us with much familiarity, as if we had formed friendship with them. Walking with them on the beach and talking, being desirous of drinking fresh water, they made signs that they had none, and offered their herb and powder; from which we concluded that the island was ill-provided with water, and that they kept this herb in their mouths to keep off thirst. We walked over the island for a day and a half, without finding a spring of water, and we saw that the water they drank was what had fallen during the night on certain leaves which looked like ass's ears, and held the water, and of this they drank. It was excellent water; and these leaves are not found in many places. They had no kind of meat, 92 and no roots, as on the mainland. They were sustained by fish caught in the sea, of which they had great abundance, and they were very good fishermen.

They gave us many turtles, and many large and excellent fish. Their women did not have the herb in their mouths like the men, but they all carried a gourd with water, from which they drank. They have no villages nor houses, but merely live under bowers of leaves, which shade them from the sun, though not from the rain. But I believe that it seldom rains on that island. When they are fishing out at sea they all have a very large leaf, and of such width that it forms a shade. As the sun rises, so they raise the leaf, and thus they protect themselves from the sun.

The island contains many animals of various sorts, and much water in swamps, and seeing that it offered no profit whatever, we departed and went to another island. We found that this other island was inhabited by very tall people. We landed to see whether there was any fresh water, and not thinking it was inhabited, as we had not seen anyone, we came upon very large foot-marks in the sand, as we were walking along the beach. We judged that if the other measurements were in proportion to those of their feet, they must be very tall. Going in search, we came into a road which led inland. There were nine of us. Judging that there could not be many inhabitants, as the island was small, we walked over it to see what sort of people they were. When we had gone 93 about a league we saw five huts, which appeared to be uninhabited, in a valley, and we went to them. But we only found five women, two old, and three children of such lofty stature that, for the wonder of the thing, we wanted to keep them. When they saw us they were so frightened that they had not the power to run away. The two old women began to invite us with words, and to set before us many things, and took us into a hut. They were taller than a large man who may well be tall, such as was Francesco degli Albizi, but better proportioned. Our intention was to take the young girls by force, and to bring them to Castille as a wonderful thing. While we were forming this design there entered by the door of the hut as many as thirty-six men, much bigger than the women, and so well made that it was a rare thing to behold them. They, in like manner, put us into such a state of perturbation that we rather wished we were on board, than having dealings with such people. They carried very large bows and arrows, and great clubs with knobs. They talked among themselves in a tone as if they wished to destroy us. Seeing ourselves in such danger, we made various suggestions one to another. Some proposed that we should attack them in the hut, and others said that it would be better to do so outside, while others advised that we should not take any action until we saw what the natives were going to do. We at last agreed to go out of the hut, and walk away in the direction of the ships as if nothing had happened, and this we did. Having taken our route to return to the ships, they also came along behind us at a distance of about a stone's-throw, talking among themselves. I believe they had not less fear of us than we of them; for sometimes we stopped to rest, and they did so also without coming nearer. At last we came to the beach, where the boats where waiting for us. We got in, and, when we were some way from the shore, the natives rushed down and shot many arrows; but we then had little fear of them. We replied with two bombard-shots, more to frighten them than to do them harm. They all fled into the woods, and so we took leave of them, thankful to escape after a dangerous adventure. They all went naked like the others. We called this island the Island of the Giants, by reason of their stature. 94

We proceeded onwards along the coast, and there happened to be combats with the natives many times, because they did not wish us to take anything from the land. At length we became desirous of returning to Castille, having been on the sea for nearly a year 95 and the provisions being nearly exhausted, the little that remained being damaged by the heat.

For from the time that we left the islands of Cape Verde until now, we had been continually navigating within the Torrid Zone, and twice we had crossed the equinoctial line; for, as I said before, we went 5° beyond it to the south, and now we were in 15° 96 to the north. Being in this state of mind, it pleased the Holy Spirit to give us some rest from our great hardships; for as we were searching for a port in which to repair our ships, we came upon a people who received us with much friendship. We found that they had a very great quantity of oriental pearls, and exceedingly good ones. We stayed with them forty-seven days, and obtained from them 119 marcs of pearls for very little merchandise in exchange. I believe the pearls did not cost us the value of forty ducats. What we gave them was nothing but bells, and looking-glasses, and beads, 97 and ten bells, and tin foil. For one bell a native gave all the pearls he had. Here we learnt how they fished for them, and where, and they gave us many shells in which they are born. We bartered for a shell in which were born 130 pearls, and in others less. This one of 130 the Queen took, and others I put aside that they might not be seen. Your Magnificence must know that if the pearls are not mature, and are not detached, they soon perish, and of this I have had experience. When they are mature, they are detached in the shell, and are placed among the flesh. These are good. When they were bad the greater part were cracked and badly bored. Nevertheless they are worth a good deal of money when sold in the market.

At the end of forty-seven days we took leave of these very friendly natives. We departed, and, for the sake of obtaining many things of which we were in need, we shaped a course for the island of Antiglia, 98 being that which Christopher Columbus discovered a few years ago. Here we took many supplies on board, and remained two months and seventeen days. 99 Here we endured many dangers and troubles from the same Christians who were in this island with Columbus. I believe this was caused by envy; but to avoid prolixity, I will refrain from recounting what happened. We departed from the said island on the 22nd of July, 100 and after a voyage of a month and a half, we entered the port of Cadiz on the 8th of September, 101 being my second voyage. God be praised.

END OF THE SECOND VOYAGE.

Evidence of Alonso De Hojeda

(Respecting his Voyage of 1499-1500).

Alonzo de Hojeda gave evidence that the true reply to the question is, that this witness is the said Hojeda, who was the first man that went to make discoveries after the said Admiral, and that he discovered the mainland to the south and coasted it for nearly 200 leagues to Paria, and went out by the "Boca del Drago", and there he knew that the Admiral had been at the island of Trinidad, near the "Boca del Drago", and that he went on and discovered the coast of the mainland as far as the Gulf of Pearls and the island of Margarita, where he landed, because he knew that the Admiral had only sighted it, and thence he proceeded to discover all the coast of the mainland from "Los Frayles" to the "Islas de los Gigantes", the Gulf of Venecia, which is on the mainland, and the provinces of Quinquilacoa. On all that land, from 200 leagues beyond Paria, and from Paria to the Pearls, and from the Pearls to Quinquilacoa, which this witness discovered, no one else had discovered or touched at, neither the Admiral nor any other person, and in this voyage the said witness took with him Juan de la Cosa and Morigo Vespuche, and other pilots, and this witness was despatched for this voyage by order of the said Don Juan de Fonseca, Bishop of Palencia, by order of their Highnesses. 102

Voyage of Hojeda, 1499-1500.
(From Navarrete, iii, pp. 3-11.)

In December 1498 the news arrived of the discovery of Paria. The splendid ideas of the discoverer touching the beauty and wealth of that region were presently made known, and the spirit of maritime enterprise was revived with renewed vigour. Some of those who had sailed with the Admiral, and had benefited by his instruction and example, solicited and obtained from the Court licences to discover, at their own proper cost, the regions beyond what was already known, paying into the Treasury a fourth or fifth part of what they acquired.

The first who adventured was Alonso de Hojeda, a native of Cuenca. Owing to his energy and the favour of the Bishop Don Rodriguez de Fonseca, he soon collected the funds and the crews necessary for the equipment of four vessels in the Port of Santa Maria, where Juan de la Cosa resided, a great mariner according to popular ideas, and not inferior to the Admiral himself in his own conceit. He had been a shipmate and pupil of the Admiral in the expedition of Cuba and Jamaica. This man was the principal pilot of Hojeda. They also engaged others who had been in the Paria voyage. Among the other sharers in the enterprise, the Florentine Americo Vespucci merits special mention. He was established in Seville, but became tired of a mercantile life, and entered upon the study of cosmography and nautical subjects, with the desire of embracing a more glorious career. Perhaps this passion was excited by intercourse with the Admiral in the house of Juan Berardi, a merchant, and also a Florentine, and owing to his having become acquainted through this house with the armaments and provisions for the Indies, so that he desired to place his services at the disposal of the commander of the present enterprise.

With such useful companions Hojeda put to sea on the 18th 103 or the 20th of May 1499. 104 They touched at the Canaries, where they took in such supplies as they needed, and entered on the ocean voyage from Gomera, following the route of the last voyage of the Admiral, for Hojeda was in possession of the marine chart which Columbus had drawn. At the end of twenty-four days they came in sight of the continent of the new world, further south than the point reached by the Admiral, and apparently on the coast of Surinam. They sailed along in sight of the coast for nearly 200 leagues, from the neighbourhood of the equator to the Gulf of Paria, without landing. In passing, besides other rivers, they saw two very large ones which made the sea water to be fresh for a long distance, one coming from south to north, which should be the river now called Essequibo in Dutch Guiana, and which was for some time called the Rio Dulce. The course of the other was from west to east, and may have been the Orinoco, the waters of which flow for many leagues into the sea without mixing with the salt water. The land on the coast was, generally, low and covered with very dense forest. The currents were exceedingly strong towards the N. E., following the general direction of the coast.

The first inhabited land seen by our navigators was the island of Trinidad, on the south coast of which they saw a crowd of astonished people watching them from the shore. They landed at three different places with the launches well provisioned, and twenty-two well-armed men. The natives were Caribs, or Cannibals, of fine presence and stature, of great vigour, and very expert in the use of bows and arrows, and shields, which were their proper arms. Although they showed some reluctance to come near the Spaniards at first, they were very soon satisfied of the friendly intentions of the strangers, and bartered with them amicably. Thence they entered the Gulf of Paria, and anchored near the river Guarapiche, where they also saw a populous village of peaceful Indians near the shore. They opened communications with the inhabitants, and, among other presents, received from them a kind of cider made of fruits, as well as some fruit like mirabolans, of exquisite flavour, and here some pearls were obtained. They saw parrots of various colours; and they parted company with these people on friendly terms. Hojeda says that they found traces of the Admiral having been in the island of Trinidad, near the Dragon's Mouth, which circumstance was carefully omitted by Vespucci.

Having passed the mouth of the terrible strait, Hojeda continued his discovery along the coast of the mainland as far as the Gulf of Pearls or Curiana, visiting and landing on the island of Margarita, which is in front, as he knew that Columbus had only sighted it in passing. In passing he noticed the islets called Los Frailes, which are nine miles to the east, and north of Margarita, and the rock Centinela. Thence he stood in shore by the cape Isleos (now called Codera), anchoring in the road which he called Aldea vencida. He continued to coast along from port to port, according to the expression of the pilot Morales, until he reached the Puerto Flechado, now Chichirivichi, where he seems to have had some encounter with the Indians, who wounded twenty-one of his men, of whom one died, as soon as he was brought to be cured, in one of the coves that are between that port and the Vela de Coro, where they remained twenty days. From this place they shaped a course for the island of Curaçoa, which they called Isla de los Gigantes, where Americo supposed there was a race of uncommon stature. Perhaps he did not understand the expressions of horror with which the natives referred to the Caribs, and this sufficed to make Vespucci assert that he had seen Pontasiloas and Antæus. 105 They then crossed to a land which they judged to be an island, distant ten leagues from Curaçoa, and saw the cape forming a peninsula, which they named San Roman, probably because it was discovered on the 9th of August, on which the feast of that saint is kept. Having rounded the cape, they entered a great gulf, on the eastern side of which, where it is shallow and clear of rocks, they saw a great village, with the houses built over the water, on piles driven into the bottom, and the people communicated from one to the other in canoes. Hojeda named it the Gulf of Venice, from its similarity to that famous city in Italy. The Indians called it the Gulf of Coquibacoa, and we know it now as the Gulf of Venezuela. They explored the interior, and discovered, as it would seem, on the 24th of August, the lake and port of San Bartolomè, 106 now the lake of Maracaibo, where they obtained some Indian women of notable beauty and disposition. It is certain that the natives of this country had the fame of being more beautiful and gracious than those of any other part of that continent. Having explored the western part of the gulf, and doubled the Cape of Coquibacoa, Hojeda and his companions examined the coast as far as the Cabo de la Vela, the extreme point reached in this voyage. On the 30th of August they turned on their homeward voyage for Española or Santo Domingo, and entered the port of Yaquimo on the 5th of September 1499, with the intention of loading with brasil wood, according to what Don Fernando Columbus says.

Here Hojeda had those disputes with Roldan which are referred to by our historians, but, finally, with leave from that chief, Hojeda removed his ships to Surana, in February 1500. 107 According to Vespucci, in his letter to Medici, 108 they navigated from Española in a northerly direction for 200 leagues, discovering more than a thousand islands, most of them inhabited, which would probably be the Lucayos, although those are not nearly so numerous. On one of these he says that they violently seized 232 persons for slaves, and that from thence they returned to Spain by the islands of the Azores, Canary and Madeira, arriving in the Bay of Cadiz in the middle of June 1500, where they sold many of the 200 slaves that arrived, the rest having died on the voyage. The truth of these events is not very certain, but it is certain that the profit of the expedition was very small. According to the same Vespucci, deducting costs, not more than 500 ducats remained to divide among 55 shareholders, and this when, besides the price of the slaves, they brought home a quantity of pearls, worthy of a place in the royal treasury, of gold and some precious stones, but not many, for, imitating badly the acts of the Admiral, the desire to push on for discovery was greater than that for the acquisition of riches.

Third Voyage of Amerigo Vespucci.

Being afterwards in Seville, resting from so many labours that I had endured during these two voyages, and intending to return to the land of pearls, Fortune showed that she was not content with these my labours. I know not how there came into the thoughts of the Most Serene King Don Manuel of Portugal the wish to have my services. But being at Seville, without any thought of going to Portugal, a messenger came to me with a letter from the Royal Crown, in which I was asked to come to Lisbon, to confer with his Highness, who promised to show me favour. I was not inclined to go, and I despatched the messenger with a reply that I was not well, but that when I had recovered, if his Highness still wished for my services, I would come as soon as he might send for me. Seeing that he could not have me, he arranged to send Giuliano di Bartolomeo di Giocondo for me, he being in Lisbon, with instructions that, come what might, he should bring me. The said Giuliano came to Seville, and prayed so hard that I was forced to go. My departure was taken ill by many who knew me, for I left Castille where honour was done me, and where the King held me in good esteem. It was worse that I went without bidding farewell to my host.

When I was presented to that King, he showed his satisfaction that I had come, and asked me to go in company with three of his ships that were ready to depart for the discovery of new lands. As the request of a king is a command, I had to consent to whatever he asked, and we sailed from this port of Lisbon with three ships on the 10th of March 1501, shaping our course direct for the island of Grand Canary. We passed without sighting it, and continued along the west coast of Africa. On this coast we made our fishery of a sort of fish called parchi. We remained three days, and then came to a port on the coast of Ethiopia called Besechiece, 109 which is within the Torrid Zone, the North Pole rising above it 14° 30′, situated in the first climate. Here we remained two days, taking in wood and water; for my intention was to shape a course towards the south, in the Atlantic Gulf. We departed from this port of Ethiopia, and steered to the south-west, taking a quarter point to the south

110 until, after sixty-seven days, we came in sight of land, which was 700 leagues from the said port to the south-west. 111 In those sixty-seven days we had the worst time that man ever endured who navigated the seas, owing to the rains, perturbations, and storms that we encountered. The season was very contrary to us, by reason of the course of our navigation being continually in contact with the equinoctial line, where, in the month of June, it is winter. We found that the day and the night were equal, and that the shadow was always towards the south.

It pleased God to show us a new land on the 17th of August, and we anchored at a distance of half a league, and got our boats out. We then went to see the land, whether it was inhabited, and what it was like. We found that it was inhabited by people who were worse than animals. But your Magnificence must understand that we did not see them at first, though we were convinced that the country was inhabited, by many signs observed by us. We took possession for that Most Serene King; and found the land to be very pleasant and fertile, and of good appearance. It was 5° to the south of the equinoctial line. We went back to the ships, and as we were in great want of wood and water, we determined, next day, to return to the shore, with the object of obtaining what we wanted. Being on shore, we saw some people at the top of a hill, who were looking at us, but without showing any intention of coming down. They were naked, and of the same colour and form as the others we had seen. We tried to induce them to come and speak with us, but did not succeed, as they would not trust us. Seeing their obstinacy, and it being late, we returned on board, leaving many bells and mirrors on shore, and other things in their sight. As soon as we were at some distance on the sea, they came down from the hill, and showed themselves to be much astonished at the things. On that day we were only able to obtain water.

Next morning we saw from the ship that the people on shore had made a great smoke, and thinking it was a signal to us, we went on shore, where we found that many people had come, but they still kept at a distance from us. They made signs to us that we should come inland with them. Two of our Christians were, therefore, sent to ask their captain for leave to go with them a short distance inland, to see what kind of people they were, and if they had any riches, spices, or drugs. The captain was contented, so they got together many things for barter, and parted from us, with instructions that they should not be more than five days absent, as we would wait that time for them. So they set out on their road inland, and we returned to the ships to wait for them. Nearly every day people came to the beach, but they would not speak with us. On the seventh day we went on shore, and found that they had arranged with their women; for, as we jumped on shore, the men of the land sent many of their women to speak with us. Seeing that they were not reassured, we arranged to send to them one of our people, who was a very agile and valiant youth. To give them more confidence, the rest of us went back into the boats. He went among the women, and they all began to touch and feel him, wondering at him exceedingly. Things being so, we saw a woman come from the hill, carrying a great stick in her hand. 112 When she came to where our Christian stood, she raised it, and gave him such a blow that he was felled to the ground. The other women immediately took him by the feet, and dragged him towards the hill. The men rushed down to the beach, and shot at us with their bows and arrows. Our people, in great fear, hauled the boats towards their anchors, 113 which were on shore; but, owing to the quantities of arrows that came into the boats, no one thought of taking up their arms. At last, four rounds from the bombard were fired at them, and they no sooner heard the report than they all ran away towards the hill, where the women were still tearing the Christian to pieces. At a great fire they had made they roasted him before our eyes, showing us many pieces, and then eating them. The men made signs how they had killed the other two Christians and eaten them. What shocked us much was seeing with our eyes the cruelty with which they treated the dead, which was an intolerable insult to all of us.

Having arranged that more than forty of us should land and avenge such cruel murder, and so bestial and inhuman an act, the principal captain would not give his consent. We departed from them unwillingly, and with much shame, caused by the decision of our captain.

We left this place, and commenced our navigation by shaping a course between east and south. Thus we sailed along the land, making many landings, seeing natives, but having no intercourse with them. We sailed on until we found that the coast made a turn to the west when we had doubled a cape, to which we gave the name of the Cape of St. Augustine. 114 We then began to shape a course to the south-west. The cape is distant from the place where the Christians were murdered 150 leagues towards the east, and this cape is 8° from the equinoctial line to the south. In navigating we saw one day a great multitude of people on the beach, gazing at the wonderful sight of our ships. As we sailed we turned the ship towards them, anchored in a good place, and went on shore with the boats. We found the people to be better conditioned than those we had met with before, and, responding to our overtures, they soon made friends, and treated with us. We were five days in this place, and found canna fistola very thick and green, and dry on the tops of the trees. We determined to take a pair of men from this place, that they might teach us their language, and three of them came voluntarily to go to Portugal.

Lest your Magnificence should be tired of so much writing, you must know that, on leaving this port, we sailed along on a westerly course, always in sight of land, continually making many landings, and speaking with an infinite number of people. We were so far south that we were outside the Tropic of Capricorn, where the South Pole rises above the horizon 32°. We had lost sight altogether of Ursa Minor and Ursa Major, which were far below and scarcely seen on the horizon. 115 We guided ourselves by the stars of the

South Pole, which are numerous and much larger and brighter than those of our Pole. I traced the figure of the greater part of those of the first magnitude, with a declaration of their orbits round the South Pole, and of their diameters and semi-diameters, as may be seen in my Four Voyages. We sailed along that coast for 750 leagues, 150 from the cape called St. Augustine, to the west, and 600 to the south.

Desiring to recount the things I saw on that coast, and what happened to us, as many more leaves would not suffice me. On the coast we saw an infinite number of trees, brazil wood 116 and cassia, and those trees which yield myrrh, as well as other marvels of nature which I am unable to recount. Having now been ten months on the voyage, and having seen that there was no mining wealth whatever in that land, we decided upon taking leave of it, and upon sailing across the sea for some other part. Having held a consultation, it was decided that the course should be taken which seemed good to me; and the command of the fleet was entrusted to me. I gave orders that the fleet should be supplied with wood and water for six months, such being the decision of the officers of the ships. Having made our departure from this land, we began our navigation with a southerly course on the 15th of February, when already the sun moved towards the equinoctial, and turned towards our Hemisphere of the North. We sailed so far on this course that we found ourselves where the South Pole had a height above our horizon of 52° and we could no longer see the stars of Ursa Minor or of Ursa Major. We were then 500 leagues to the south of the port whence we had departed, and this was on the 3rd of April. On this day such a tempest arose on the sea that all our sails were blown away, and we ran under bare poles, with a heavy southerly gale and a tremendous sea; the air being very tempestuous. The gale was such that all the people in the fleet were much alarmed. The nights were very long, for the night we had on the 7th of April lasted fifteen hours, the sun being at the end of Aries, and in that region it was winter, as your Magnificence will be well aware. Sailing in this storm, on the 7th of April we came in sight of new land, 117 along which we ran for nearly 20 leagues, and found it all a rocky coast, without any port or inhabitants. I believe this was because the cold was so great that no one in the fleet could endure it. Finding ourselves in such peril, and in such a storm that we could scarcely see one ship from another, owing to the greatness of the waves and the blinding mist, it was agreed with the principal captain that a signal should be made to the ships that they should make for land, and then shape a course for Portugal. This was very good counsel, for it is certain that if we had delayed another night all would have been lost; for, as we wore round on the next day, we were met by such a storm that we expected to be swamped. We had to undertake pilgrimages and perform other ceremonies, as is the custom of sailors at such times. We ran for five days, always coming towards the equinoctial line, where the air and sea became more temperate. It pleased God to deliver us from such peril. Our course was now between the north and north-east, for our intention was to reach the coast of Ethiopia, our distance from it being 300 leagues, in the Gulf of the Atlantic Sea. By the grace of God, on the 10th day of May, we came in sight of land, where we were able to refresh ourselves, the land being called La Serra Liona. We were there fifteen days, and thence shaped a course to the islands of the Azores, which are distant nearly 750 leagues from that Serra. We reached the islands in the end of July, where we remained fifteen days taking some recreation. Thence we departed for Lisbon, distant 300 leagues to the west, and arrived at that port of Lisbon on the 7th of September 1502, may God be thanked for our salvation, with only two ships. We burnt the other at Serra Liona, because she was no longer seaworthy. We were employed on this voyage nearly fifteen months; and for eleven days we navigated without seeing the North Star, nor the Great or Little Bears, which they call el corno, and we were guided by the stars of the other Pole. This is what I saw on this voyage.

Letter on his Third Voyage from Amerigo Vespucci to Lorenzo Pietro Francesco di Medici.

March (or April) 1503.

Alberico Vesputio to Lorenzo Pietro di Medici, salutation. In passed days I wrote very fully to you of my return from the new countries, which have been found and explored with the ships, at the cost, and by the command, of this Most Serene King of Portugal; and it is lawful to call it a new world, because none of these countries were known to our ancestors, and to all who hear about them they will be entirely new. For the opinion of the ancients was, that the greater part of the world beyond the equinoctial line to the south was not land, but only sea, which they have called the Atlantic; and if they have affirmed that any continent is there, they have given many reasons for denying that it is inhabited. But this their opinion is false, and entirely opposed to the truth. My last voyage has proved it, for I have found a continent in that southern part; more populous and more full of animals than our Europe, or Asia, or Africa, and even more temperate and pleasant than any other region known to us, as will be explained further on. I shall write succinctly of the principal things only, and the things most worthy of notice and of being remembered, which I either saw or heard of in this new world, as presently will become manifest.

We set out, on a prosperous voyage, on the 14th of May 118 1501, sailing from Lisbon, by order of the aforesaid King, with three ships, to discover new countries towards the west; and we sailed towards the south continuously for twenty months. 119 Of this navigation the order is as follows: Our course was for the Fortunate Islands, so called formerly, but now we call them the Grand Canary Islands, which are in the third climate, and on the confines of the inhabited west. Thence we sailed rapidly over the ocean along the coast of Africa and part of Ethiopia to the Ethiopic Promontory, so called by Ptolemy, which is now called Cape Verde, and by the Ethiopians Biseghier, and that country Mandraga, 13° within the Torrid Zone, on the north side of the equinoctial line. The country is inhabited by a black race. Having taken on board what we required, we weighed our anchors and made sail, taking our way across the vast ocean towards the Antarctic Pole, with some westing. From the day when we left the before-mentioned promontory, we sailed for the space of two months and three days. 120 Hitherto no land had appeared to us in that vast sea. In truth, how much we had suffered, what dangers of shipwreck, I leave to the judgment of those to whom the experience of such things is very well known. What a thing it is to seek unknown lands, and how difficult, being ignorant, to narrate briefly what happened. It should be known that, of the sixty-seven days of our voyage, we were navigating continuously forty-four. We had copious thunderstorms and perturbations, and it was so dark that we never could see either the sun in the day or the moon at night. This caused us great fear, so that we lost all hope of life. In these most terrible dangers of the sea it pleased the Most High to show us the continent and the new countries, being another unknown world. These things being in sight, we were as much rejoiced as anyone may imagine who, after calamity and ill-fortune, has obtained safety.

It was on the 7th August 121 1501, that we reached those countries, thanking our Lord God with solemn prayers, and celebrating a choral Mass. We knew that land to be a continent, and not an island, from its long beaches extending without trending round, the infinite number of inhabitants, the numerous tribes and peoples, the numerous kinds of wild animals unknown in our country, and many others never seen before by us, touching which it would take long to make reference. The clemency of God was shown forth to us by being brought to these regions; for the ships were in a leaking state, and in a few days our lives might have been lost in the sea. To Him be the honour and glory, and the grace of the action.

We took counsel, and resolved to navigate along the coast of this continent towards the east, and never to lose sight of the land. We sailed along until we came to a point where the coast turned to the south. The distance from the landfall to this point was nearly 300 leagues. 122 In this stretch of coast we often landed, and had friendly relations with the natives, 123 as I shall presently relate. I had forgotten to tell you that from Cape Verde to the first land of this continent the distance is nearly 700 leagues; although I estimate that we went over more than 1,800, partly owing to ignorance of the route, and partly owing to the tempests and foul winds which drove us off our course, and sent us in various directions. If my companions had not trusted in me, to whom cosmography was known, no one, not the leader of our navigation, would have known where we were after running 500 leagues. We were wandering and full of errors, and only the instruments for taking the altitudes of heavenly bodies showed us our position. These were the quadrant and astrolabe, as known to all. These have been much used by me with much honour; for I showed them that a knowledge of the marine chart, and the rules taught by it, are more worth than all the pilots in the world. For these pilots have no knowledge beyond those places to which they have often sailed. Where the said point of land showed us the trend of the coast to the south, we agreed to continue our voyage, and to ascertain what there might be in those regions. We sailed along the coast for nearly 500 leagues, often going on shore and having intercourse with the natives, who received us in a brotherly manner. We sometimes stayed with them for fifteen or twenty days continuously, as friends and guests, as I shall relate presently. Part of this continent is in the Torrid Zone, beyond the equinoctial line towards the South Pole. But it begins at 8° beyond the equinoctial. We sailed along the coast so far that we crossed the Tropic of Capricorn, and found ourselves where the Antarctic Pole was 50° above our horizon. We went towards the Antarctic Circle until we were 17° 30′ from it 124; all which I have seen, and I have known the nature of those people, their customs, the resources and fertility of the land, the salubrity of the air, the positions of the celestial bodies in the heavens, and, above all, the fixed stars, over an eighth of the sphere, never seen by our ancestors, as I shall explain below.

As regards the people: we have found such a multitude in those countries that no one could enumerate them, as we read in the Apocalypse. They are people gentle and tractable, and all of both sexes go naked, not covering any part of their bodies, just as they came from their mothers' wombs, and so they go until their deaths. They have large, square-built bodies, and well proportioned. Their colour reddish, which I think is caused by their going naked and exposed to the sun. Their hair is plentiful and black. They are agile in walking, and of quick sight. They are of a free and good-looking expression of countenance, which they themselves destroy by boring the nostrils and lips, the nose and ears; nor must you believe that the borings are small, nor that they only have one, for I have seen those who had no less than seven borings in the face, each one the size of a plum. They stop up these perforations with blue stones, bits of marble, of crystal, or very fine alabaster, also with very white bones and other things artificially prepared according to their customs; which, if you could see, it would appear a strange and monstrous thing. One had in the nostrils and lips alone seven stones, of which some were half a palm in length. It will astonish you to hear that I considered that the weight of seven such stones was as much as sixteen ounces. In each ear they had three perforations bored, whence they had other stones and rings suspended. This custom is only for the men, as the women do not perforate their faces, but only their ears. Another custom among them is sufficiently shameful, and beyond all human credibility. Their women, being very libidinous, make the penis of their husbands swell to such a size as to appear deformed; and this is accomplished by a certain artifice, being the bite of some poisonous animal, and by reason of this many lose their virile organ and remain eunuchs.

They have no cloth, either of wool, flax, or cotton, because they have no need of it; nor have they any private property, everything being in common. They live amongst themselves without a king or ruler, each man being his own master, and having as many wives as they please. The children cohabit with the mothers, the brothers with the sisters, the male cousins with the female, and each one with the first he meets. They have no temples and no laws, nor are they idolaters. What more can I say! They live according to nature, and are more inclined to be Epicurean than Stoic. They have no commerce among each other, and they wage war without art or order. The old men make the youths do what they please, and incite them to fights, in which they mutually kill with great cruelty. They slaughter those who are captured, and the victors eat the vanquished; for human flesh is an ordinary article of food among them. You may be the more certain of this, because I have seen a man eat his children and wife; and I knew a man who was popularly credited to have eaten 300 human bodies. I was once in a certain city for twenty-seven days, where human flesh was hung up near the houses, in the same way as we expose butcher's meat. I say further that they were surprised that we did not eat our enemies, and use their flesh as food, for they say it is excellent. Their arms are bows and arrows, and when they go to war they cover no part of their bodies, being in this like beasts. We did all we could to persuade them to desist from their evil habits, and they promised us to leave off. The women, as I have said, go naked, and are very libidinous, yet their bodies are comely; but they are as wild as can be imagined.

They live for 150 years, and are rarely sick. If they are attacked by a disease they cure themselves with the roots of some herbs. These are the most noteworthy things I know about them.

The air in this country is temperate and good, as we were able to learn from their accounts that there are never any pestilences or epidemics caused by bad air. Unless they meet with violent deaths, their lives are long. I believe this is because a southerly wind is always blowing, a south wind to them being what a north wind is to us. They are expert fishermen, and the sea is full of all kinds of fish. They are not hunters; I think because here there are many kinds of wild animals, principally lions and bears, innumerable serpents, and other horrible creatures and deformed beasts; also because there are vast forests and trees of immense size. They have not the courage to face such dangers naked and without any defence.

The land is very fertile, abounding in many hills and valleys, and in large rivers, and is irrigated by very refreshing springs. It is covered with extensive and dense forests, which are almost impenetrable, and full of every kind of wild beast. Great trees grow without cultivation, of which many yield fruits pleasant to the taste and nourishing to the human body; and a great many have an opposite effect. The fruits are unlike those in our country; and there are innumerable different kinds of fruits and herbs, of which they make bread and excellent food. They also have many seeds unlike ours. No kind of metal has been found except gold, in which the country abounds, though we have brought none back in this our first navigation. The natives, however, assured us that there was an immense quantity of gold underground, and nothing was to be had from them for a price. Pearls abound, as I wrote to you.

If I was to attempt to write of all the species of animals, it would be a long and tedious task. I believe certainly that our Pliny did not touch upon a thousandth part of the animals and birds that exist in this region; nor could an artist such as Policletus, 125 succeed in painting them. All the trees are odoriferous, and some of them emit gums, oils, or other liquors. If they were our property, I do not doubt but that they would be useful to man. If the terrestrial paradise is in some part of this land, it cannot be very far from the coast we visited. It is, as I have told you, in a climate where the air is temperate at noon, being neither cold in winter nor hot in summer.

The sky and air are serene during a great part of the year. Thick vapours, with fine rain falling, last for three or four hours and then disappear like smoke. The sky is adorned with most beautiful signs and figures, in which I have noted as many as twenty stars as bright as we sometimes see Venus and Jupiter. I have considered the orbits and motions of these stars, and I have measured the circumference and diameters of the stars by a geometrical method, 126 ascertaining which were the largest. I saw in the heaven three Canopi, two certainly bright, and the other obscure. The Antarctic Pole is not figured with a Great Bear and a Little Bear, like our Arctic Pole, nor is any bright star seen near it, and of those which go round in the shortest circuit there are three which have the figure of the orthogonous triangle, of which the smallest has a diameter of 9 half-degrees. To the east of these is seen a Canopus of great size, and white, which, when in mid-heaven, has this figure:—

```
        *                        s s
                               s s s s
                             s s s s s s
                               s s s s
                                            canopus
        *                        *
```

After these come two others, of which the half-circumference, the diameter, has 12 half-degrees; and with them is seen another Canopus. To these succeed six other most beautiful and very bright stars, beyond all the others of the eighth sphere, which, in the superficies of the heaven, have half the circumference, the diameter 32°, and with them is one black Canopus of immense size, seen in the Milky Way, and they have this shape when they are on the meridian:—

```
                              *
     *     *     *                           *
                       s s
                    s s s s s
                    s s s s s s
                      s s s
                       *
```

I have known many other very beautiful stars, which I have diligently noted down, and have described very well in a certain little book describing this my navigation, which at present is in the possession of that Most Serene King, and I hope he will restore it to me. In that hemisphere I have seen things not compatible with the opinions of philosophers. Twice I have seen a white rainbow towards the middle of the night, which was not only observed by me, but also by all the sailors. Likewise we often saw the new moon on the day on which it is in conjunction with the sun. Every night, in that part of the heavens of which we speak, there were innumerable vapours and burning meteors. I have told you, a little way back, that, in the hemisphere of which we are speaking, it is not a complete hemisphere in respect to ours, because it does not take that form so that it may be properly called so.

Therefore, as I have said, from Lisbon, whence we started, the distance from the equinoctial line is 39°, and we navigated beyond the equinoctial line to 50°, which together make 90°, which is one quarter of a great circle, according to the true measurement handed down to us by the ancients, so that it is manifest that we must have navigated over a fourth part of the earth. By this reasoning, we who inhabit Lisbon, at a distance of 39° from the equinoctial line in north latitude, are to those who live under 50° beyond the same line, in meridional length, angularly 5° on a transverse line. I will explain this more clearly: a perpendicular line, while we stand upright, if suspended from a point of the heavens exactly vertical, hangs over our heads; but it hangs over them sideways. Thus, while we are on a right line, they are on a transverse line. An orthogonal triangle is thus formed, of which we

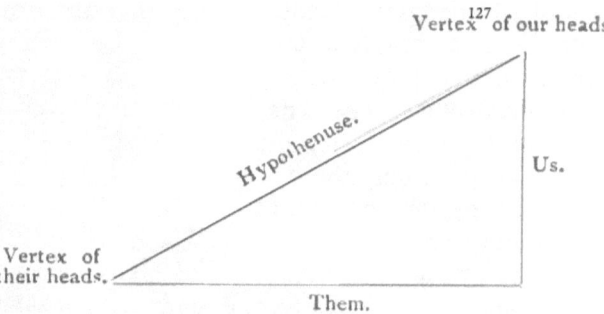

Vertex[127] of our heads.

Hypothenuse.

Us.

Vertex of their heads.

Them.

have the right line, but the base and hypotenuse to them seems the vertical line, as in this figure it will appear. This will suffice as regards cosmography.

These are the most notable things that I have seen in this my last navigation, or, as I call it, the third voyage. For the other two voyages were made by order of the Most Serene King of Spain to the west, in which I noted many wonderful works of God, our Creator; and if I should have time, I intend to collect all these singular and wonderful things into a geographical or cosmographical book, that my record may live with future generations; and the immense work of the omnipotent God will be known, in parts still unknown, but known to us. I also pray that the most merciful God will prolong my life that, with His good grace, I may be able to make the best disposition of this my wish. I keep the other two journeys in my sanctuary, and the Most Serene King restoring to me the third journey, I intend to return to peace and my country. There, in consultation with learned persons, and comforted and aided by friends, I shall be able to complete my work.

I ask your pardon for not having sooner been able to send you this my last navigation, as I had promised in my former letters. I believe that you will understand the cause, which was that I could not get the books from this Most Serene King. I think of undertaking a fourth voyage in the same direction, and promise is already made of two ships with their armaments, in which I may seek new regions of the East on a course called Africus. In which journey I hope much to do God honour, to be of service to this kingdom, to secure repute for my old age, and I expect no other result with the permission of this Most Serene King. May God permit what is for the best, and you shall be informed of what happens.

This letter was translated from the Italian into the Latin language by Jocundus, interpreter, as everyone understands Latin who desires to learn about these voyages, and to search into the things of heaven, and to know all that is proper to be known; for, from the time the world began, so much has not been discovered touching the greatness of the earth and what is contained in it.

Fourth Voyage of Amerigo Vespucci.

It remains for me to relate the things I saw in the fourth voyage; but as I am already tired, and as the voyage did not end as was intended, owing to an accident which happened in the Atlantic, as your Magnificence will shortly understand, I propose to be brief. We departed from this port of Lisbon with six ships, 128 having the intention of discovering an island in the East called Melaccha, of which it was reported that it was very rich, and that it was the mart of all the ships that navigate the Gangetic and Indian Seas, as Cadiz is the mart for all vessels passing from east to west or from west to east by way of Galicut. This Melaccha is more to the west than Galicut, and much more to the south, for we know that it is in 33° from the Antarctic Pole. 129 We departed on the 10th of May 1503, and shaped a course direct for the Cape Verde Islands, where we careened and took in fresh provisions, remaining for thirteen days. Thence we continued on our voyage, shaping a south-easterly course, and as our commander was a presumptuous and very obstinate man, he wanted to go to Serra-liona, in the southern land of Æthiopia, without any necessity, unless it was to show that he was commander of the six ships, and he acted against the wishes of all the other captains. Thus navigating, when we came in sight of the said land the weather was so bad, with a contrary wind, that we were in sight for four days without being able to reach the place, owing to the storm. The consequence was that we were obliged to resume our proper course, and give up the said Serra, shaping a south-west course. When we had sailed for 300 leagues, being 3° to the south of the equinoctial line, a land was sighted 130 at a distance of twenty-two leagues, at which we were astonished. We found that it was an island in the midst of the sea, very high and wonderful in its formation, for it was not more than two leagues long and one broad, and uninhabited. It was an evil island for all the fleet, because your Magnificence must know that, through the bad advice and management of our commander, his ship was lost. For, with three in company, he struck on a rock in the night of St. Lawrence, which is on the 10th of August, and went to the bottom, nothing being saved but the crew. She was a ship of 300 tons, and the chief importance of the fleet centred in her. As the other ships were worn and needed repairs, the commander ordered me to go to the island in my ship, and find a good anchorage where the fleet could anchor. As my boat, with nine of my sailors, was employed in helping the other ships, he did not wish that I should take it, but that I should go without it, telling me that I should go by myself. I left the fleet in accordance with my orders, without a boat and with less than half my sailors, and went to the island, which was at a distance of four leagues. I found an excellent port where the fleet could anchor in perfect security. Here I waited for my captain and the fleet for eight days, but they never came. We were very discontented, and the men were full of apprehensions which I could not remove. Being in this state of anxiety, at last, on the eighth day, we saw a ship coming from seaward, and, fearing that she might not see us, we came out to her, expecting that she was bringing my boat and people. When we came up to her, after salutes, they told us that the Capitana was gone to the bottom, the crew being saved, and that my boat and people remained with the fleet, which had gone to that sea ahead, which was a great trouble to us. What will your Magnificence think of my finding myself 1,000 leagues from Lisbon with few men? Nevertheless, we put a bold face on the matter, and still went ahead. We returned to the island, and filled up with wood and water by using our consort's boat. We found the island to be uninhabited, supplied with abundance of fresh water, quantities of trees, and full of marine and land birds without number. They were so tame that they allowed us to take them with our hands. We caught so many that we loaded a boat with these animals. We saw nothing but very large rats, lizards with two tails, and some serpents.

Having got in our provisions we departed, shaping a course between south and south-west, for we had an order from the King that any ship parted from the rest of the fleet, or from the Commander-in-Chief, should make for the land that was visited in the previous voyage. We discovered a port to which we gave the name of the Bay of All Saints, 131 and it pleased God to give us such fine weather that we reached it in seventeen days, being 300 leagues from the island. Here we neither found our commander nor any of the other ships of the fleet. We waited in this port for two months and four days, and, seeing that there was no arrival, I and my consort determined to explore the coast. We sailed onwards for 260 leagues until we reached a harbour where we agreed to build a fort. We did so, and left twenty-four Christian men in it who were on board my consort, being part of the crew of the Capitana that was lost. We were in that harbour five months, building the fort, and loading our ships with brazil-wood. For we were not able to advance further, because we had not full crews, and I wanted many necessaries. Having done all this, we agreed to return to Portugal, which bore between north-east and north. We left the twenty-four men in the fort, with provisions for six months, twelve bombards, and many other arms. We had made friends with all the natives round, of whom I have made no mention in this voyage, not because we did not see and have intercourse with an infinite number of tribes: for we went inland with thirty men, for a distance of 40 leagues, and saw so many things that I refrain from recounting them, reserving them for my Four Voyages. This land is 18° to the south of the equinoctial line, and beyond the meridian of Lisbon 37° further to the west, according to what was shown by our instruments. All this being done, we took leave of the Christians and of that land, and began our navigation to the north-north-east, with the object of shaping a course for this city of Lisbon. After seventy-seven days of many hardships and dangers we entered this port on the 18th of June 1504. God be praised. Here we were very well received, more so than anyone would believe. For all the city had given us up, all the other ships of the fleet having been lost, owing to the pride and folly of our commander. 132 May God reward him for his pride!

At present I may be found in Lisbon, not knowing what the King may wish to do with me, but I greatly desire rest.

The bearer of this is Benvenuto di Domenico Benvenuti, who will tell your Magnificence of my condition, and of some things which I have left out to avoid prolixity, for he has seen and heard, God knows, how much of them. I have condensed the letter as much as possible, and to this end have omitted many natural things, for which your Magnificence will pardon me. I beseech you to include me in the number of your servants, and I commend you to Ser Antonio Vespucci my brother, and to all my house. I conclude praying God that He will prolong your life, and that He will favour the state of that exalted Republic and the honour of your Magnificence.

Given in Lisbon, September 4th, 1504.

Your servant,
Amerigo Vespucci, in Lisbon.

Letter from the Admiral Christopher Columbus to his Son, referring to Amerigo Vespucci.

133

My Dear Son,—Diego Mendez left here on Monday, the 3rd of this month. After his departure, I spoke with Amerigo Vespucci, the bearer of this letter, who is going to the Court on matters relating to navigation. He always showed a desire to please me, and is a very respectable man. Fortune has been adverse to him, as to many others. His labours have not been so profitable to him as he might have expected. He leaves me with the desire to do me service, if it should be in his power. I am unable here to point out in what way he could be useful to me, because I do not know what may be required at Court; but he goes with the determination of doing all he can for me. You will see in what way he can be employed. Think the matter over, as he will do everything, and speak, and put things in train; but let all be done secretly, so as not to arouse suspicion of him. I have told him all I can about my affairs, and of the payments that have been made to me and are due. This letter is also for the Adelantado, for he can see in what way use can be made of it, and will apprise you of it, etc., etc.

Dated in Seville, the 5th of February (1505).

S.
S. A. S.
X. M. Y.
XPO FERENS.

Letter from Hieronimo Vianelo to the Seigneury of Venice.

134
Burgos, December 23rd, 1506.

The two ships have arrived from the Indies, belonging to the King, my Lord, which went on a voyage of discovery under Juan Biscaino 135 and Almerigo Fiorentino. 136 They went to the S.W., 800 leagues beyond the island of Española, which is 2,000 leagues from the Straits of Hercules, and discovered mainland, which they judge to be 200 leagues from the land of Española, and after coasting along it for 600 leagues they came to a great river, with a mouth 40 leagues across, and went up it for 150 leagues, in which there are many islets inhabited by Indians. They live, for the most part, very miserably on fish, and go naked. Thence they went back with some of these Indians, and went along the coast of the said land for 600 leagues, where they met an Indian canoe, which is carved out of one piece of wood. It had a sail, and went to the mainland with eighty men, with many bows, and targets of a very light but strong wood. They went to the mainland to take Indians who live there, who do not serve them as slaves, but are eaten by them like deer, rabbits, and other animals. Our people took these Indians. Their bows are made of ebony and their arrows have corals made of the nerves of snakes. Having taken this canoe, they returned to the said island, where there came against them a great number of Indians, with bows and arrows in

54

their hands. They defeated these natives and explored the island, which they found very sterile. At noon they came to a plain, which was so covered with serpents and snakes and dragons, that it was marvellous. They kept one, as it seemed to them to be a very wonderful thing. This dragon was larger than a cachalote. 137

The island is intersected by a mountain, one part to the north the other to the south. The north side is inhabited by these Indians, the other side by those poisonous animals. They say that none of these serpents ever pass to the inhabited part, and in the whole of that side there are no serpents, nor any similar animals. Having seen this, the said ships departed, and took away seven Indians of that land, good sailors, and coasted along the coast to a place called Alseshij, and thence for 400 leagues to the westward, when they came to a land where they found many houses, out of which came many Indians to receive them and do them honour, and they say that one of these had previously predicted that certain ships of a great king, to them unknown, would come from the east and make them all slaves, and that all the strangers were gifted with life eternal, and that their persons would be adorned with various dresses. They say that when their king saw our ships he said: "Behold, here are the ships that I told you of ten years ago." This king came with a breast-plate of massive gold on his breast and a chain of gold, and a mask of gold with four golden bells of a mark each at his feet; and with him came twenty Indians, all with gold masks on their faces, beating golden kettle-drums, each weighing thirty marks. When they saw the islanders with the Spaniards they began to be disdainful, and to fight fiercely with our people with poisoned arrows. They numbered 5,000, and 140 of our men had landed. They fell to and cut to pieces nearly 700 natives, one of ours being killed by an arrow. They came to the houses, and took those masks and bells, and arms of the said king, and 800 marks of gold. They set fire to the houses, and were there ninety-six days, because the three ships that remained were sunk and went to the bottom. Seeing this, they took out the provisions and stores, and fortified themselves on shore with a very good tower. Every day they fought with the Indians. At night they were within their enclosure, and in the day they went out in order, and as much as they marched, so much they acquired. But they did not dare to go out of their quarters. One day they went to a lake, and began to wash the earth with certain vernicali, 138 each one in half an hour getting six, seven, or eight castellanos of gold. They were told by some of the Indian prisoners that they need not tire themselves with washing, for that from there to a very high mountain the distance was half a league, and that in a plain near there was a river, where it is not necessary to wash much, for each man in a day can gather ten marks of gold with little trouble. At length, as lost men, without hope of returning home, they repaired the ships and boats that were run up on the beach, eventually determining to return to Spain. During the time of ninety-six days that they were there several died from sickness, and there were forty-four survivors who were saved with the help of God. They left ten men in the tower, supplied with provisions and stores for a year, who were attacked three times by Indians with their canoes, but were always victorious, and have come safely here to the Court. I have seen all that gold and various things that they have brought back; another kind of pepper, but larger than ours, and nuts like nutmegs. They have also brought seventy pearls, all good green ones, and some of ten and twelve carats, round, and like 139 Indian pearls bored in the middle. They have also found and brought a green stone like jasper, four fingers in length, and others worn on the lips of the people. They are generally without beards.

The Archbishop intends to send the said two captains, with eight ships and four hundred men, very well furnished with arms, artillery, etc.

Royal Letter of Naturalization in the Kingdoms of Castille and Leon in favour of Vespucci. 140

Doña Juana by the Grace of God:—To do good and show grace to you, Amerigo Vespucci, Florentine, in recognition of your fidelity and of certain good service you have done, and which I expect that you will do from henceforward, by this present I make you a native of these my kingdoms of Castille and of Leon, and that you may be able to hold any public offices that you may have been given or charged with, and that you may be able to enjoy and may enjoy all the honours, favours, and liberties, pre-eminences, prerogatives and immunities, and all other things, and each one of them, which you would be able or would be bound to have and enjoy if you were born in these kingdoms and lordships.

By this my letter, and by its duplicate signed by a public notary, I order the most illustrious Prince Don Carlos, my very dear and well-beloved son, and the Infants, Dukes, Prelates, Counts, Marquises, Ricos-Hombres, Masters of the Orders, those of my Council, the judges of my courts, the magistrates of my house and court, the friars, commanders and sub-commanders of the orders, governors of castles and forts, the councillors, governors, assistant-governors, officers, knights, esquires, and citizens of all my cities, towns, and villages of these my kingdoms and lordships, and all others my subjects, of whatsoever condition, pre-eminence, or dignity they be or may be, that they shall consider you as a native of these my kingdoms and lordships, as if you had been born and brought up in them, and leave you to hold such public and royal offices and posts as may be given and entrusted to you, and such other things as you shall have an interest in, the same as if you had been born and bred in these kingdoms; and they shall maintain and cause to maintain the said honours, favours, freedoms, liberties, exemptions, pre-eminences, prerogatives and immunities, and all other things, and each one of them, that you may or ought to have and enjoy, being native of these the said my kingdoms and lordships, and that neither on them nor on any part of them shall they place, or consent to be placed, any impediment against you.

Thus I order that it shall be done, any laws or ordinances of these my kingdoms to the contrary notwithstanding, as to which or to each of them of my proper motion and certain knowledge, and absolute royal power, such as I choose to use as Queen and Natural Lady of this part, I dispense so far as they touch these presents, leaving them in force and vigour for all other things henceforward.

Given in the city of Toro, on the 24th day of April, in the year of the birth of our Lord Jesus Christ, 1505 years. I, the King.

I, Gaspar de Goicio, Licentiate Zapata, Licenciate Polanco.

Appointment of Amerigo Vespucci as Chief Pilot.
Doña Juana:—Seeing that it has come to our notice, and that we have seen by experience, that, owing to the pilots not being so expert as is necessary, nor so well instructed in what they ought to know, so as to be competent to rule and govern the ships that navigate in the voyage over the Ocean Sea to our islands and mainland which we possess in the Indies; and that through their default, either in not knowing how to rule and govern, or through not knowing how to find the altitude by the quadrant or astrolabe, nor the methods of calculating it, have happened many disasters, and those who have sailed under their governance have been exposed to great danger, by which our Lord has been ill-served, as well as our finances, while the merchants who trade thither have received much hurt and loss. And for a remedy to the above, and because it is necessary, as well for that navigation as for other voyages by which, with the help of our Lord, we hope to make new discoveries in other lands, that there should be persons who are more expert and better instructed, and who know the things necessary for such navigation, so that those who are under them may go more safely, it is our will and pleasure, and we order that all the pilots of our kingdoms and lordships, who are now or shall hereafter be appointed as pilots in the said navigation to the islands and mainland that we possess in the parts of the Indies, and in other parts of the Ocean Sea, shall be instructed and shall know what it is necessary for them to know respecting the quadrant and astrolabe, in order that, by uniting theory with practice, they may be able to make good use of them in the said voyages made to the said parts, and, without such knowledge, no one shall go in the said ships as pilots, nor receive pay as pilots, nor may the masters receive them on board ship, until they have first been examined by you, Amerigo Despuchi, our Chief Pilot, and they shall be given by you a certificate of examination and approval touching the knowledge of each one. Holding the said certificates, we order that they shall be taken and received as expert pilots by whoever is shown them, for it is our pleasure that you shall be examiner of the said pilots.

In order that those who have not the knowledge may more easily learn, we order that you are to teach them, in your house in Seville, all those things that they ought to know, you receiving payment for your trouble. And as it may happen that now, in the beginning, there may be a scarcity of passed pilots, and some ships may be detained for the want of them, causing loss and harm to the citizens of the said islands, as well as to merchants and other persons who trade thither, we order you, the said Amerigo, and we give you licence that you may select the most efficient pilots from among those who have been there, that for one or two voyages, or for a certain period, they may supply what is necessary, while those others acquire the knowledge that they have to learn, so that there may be time for them to learn what is needed.

It is also reported to us that there are many charts, by different masters, on which are delineated the lands and islands of the Indies, to us belonging, which by our order have recently been discovered, and that these charts differ very much one from another, as well in the routes as in the delineations of coasts, which may cause much inconvenience. In order that there may be uniformity, it is our pleasure, and we order that there shall be made a general chart (Padron General), and that it may be more accurate, we order our officers of the House of Contratacion at Seville that they shall assemble all the ablest pilots that are to be found in the country at the time, and that, in the presence of you, Amerigo Despuchi, our Chief Pilot, a padron of all the lands and islands of the Indies that have hitherto been discovered belonging to our kingdoms and lordships shall be made; and that for it, after consulting and reasoning with those pilots, and in accord with you, the said Chief Pilot, a general padron shall be constructed, which shall be called the Padron Real, by which all pilots shall be ruled and governed, and that it shall be in the possession of the aforesaid our officers, and of you, our Chief Pilot; and that no pilot shall use any other chart, but only one which has been taken from the Padron Real, on pain of a fine of fifty dobles towards the works of the House of Contratacion of the Indies in the city of Seville.

We further order all the pilots of our kingdoms and lordships who, from this time forward, shall go to the said our lands of the Indies, discovered or to be discovered, that, when they find new lands, islands, bays, or harbours, or anything else, that they make a note of them for the said Padron Real, and on arriving in Castille that they shall give an account to you, the said our Chief Pilot, and to the officers of the House of Contratacion of Seville, that all may be delineated properly on the said Padron Real, with the object that navigators may be better taught and made expert in navigation. We further order that none of our pilots who navigate the Ocean Sea, from this time forward, shall go without their quadrant and astrolabe and the rules for working them, under the penalty that those who do not comply be rendered incompetent to exercise the said employment during our pleasure, and they shall not resume such employment without our special licence, paying a fine of 10,000 maravedis towards the works of the said House of Contratacion at Seville. Amerigo Despuchi shall use and exercise the said office of our Chief Pilot, and you are empowered to do so, and you shall do all the things contained in this letter, and which appertain to the said office; and by this our letter, and by its copy attested by the public notary, we order the Prince Charles, our very dear and well-beloved son, the Infantes, Dukes, Prelates, Counts, Marquises, Ricos-Hombres, Masters of Orders, Members of Council, and Judges of our Courts and Chancelleries, and the other priors, commanders, sub-commanders, castellans of our castles and forts, the magistrates, officers of justice, knights, esquires, officers, and good men of all the cities, towns, and villages of our kingdoms and lordships, and all captains of ships, master mariners, pilots, mates, and all other persons whom our letter concerns or may concern, that you have and hold as our Chief Pilot, and consent and allow him to hold the said office, and to do and comply with all the things in this our letter or appertaining to it; and for their accomplishment and execution give all the favour and help that is needful for all that is here, and for each part of it; and that the above may come to the knowledge of all, and that none may pretend ignorance, we order that this our letter shall be read before the public notary, in the markets and open spaces, and other accustomed places in the said city of Seville, and in the city of Cadiz, and in all the other cities, towns, and villages of these kingdoms and lordships; and if hereafter any person or persons act against it, the said justices shall execute upon them the penalties contained in this letter, so that the above shall be observed and shall take effect without fail; and if the one or the others do not so comply, they shall be subject to a fine of 10,000 maravedis for our chamber. Further we order the man to whom this letter shall be shown, that he shall appear before us in our Court, wherever we may be for fifteen following days under the said penalty, for which we order whatever public notary may be called for this, shall give testimony signed with his seal, that we may know that our order has been executed.

Given in the city of Valladolid, the 6th of August, in the year of the birth of the Lord Jesus Christ, 1508. I, the King.

I, Lope Cunchillos, Secretary to the Queen our Lady, caused this to be written by order of the King her father. Witnessed: The Bishop of Palencia; Licentiate Ximenes.

Las Casas on The Alleged First Voyage of Amerigo Vespucci.

Chapter CXL.

It is manifest that the Admiral Don Cristobal Colon was the first by whom Divine Providence ordained that this, our great continent should be discovered, and chose him for the instrument through whom all these hitherto unknown Indies should be shown to the world. He saw it on Wednesday, the 1st of August, one day after he discovered the island of Trinidad, in the year of our salvation, 1498. 141 He gave it the name of Isla Santa, believing that it was an island. He then began to enter the Gulf of La Bellena, by the entrance called the mouth of the Serpent by him, finding all the water fresh, and it is this entrance which forms the island of Trinidad, separating it from the mainland called Santa. On the following Friday, being the 3rd of August, he discovered the point of Paria, which he also believed to be an island, giving it the name of Gracia. But all was mainland, as in due time appeared, and still more clearly now is it known that here there is an immense continent.

It is well here to consider the injury and injustice which that Americo Vespucio appears to have done to the Admiral, or that those have done who published his Four Navigations, in attributing the discovery of this continent to himself, without mentioning anyone but himself. Owing to this, all the foreigners who write of these Indies in Latin, or in their own mother-tongue, or who make charts or maps, call the continent America, as having been first discovered by Americo.

For as Americo was a Latinist, and eloquent, he knew how to make use of the first voyage he undertook, and to give the credit to himself, as if he had been the principal captain of it. He was only one of those who were with the captain, Alonso de Hojeda, either as a mariner, or because, as a trader, he had contributed towards the expenses of the expedition; but he secured notoriety by dedicating his Navigations to King Rènè of Naples. 142 Certainly these Navigations unjustly usurp from the Admiral the honour and privilege of having been the first who, by his labours, industry, and the sweat of his brow, gave to Spain and to the world a knowledge of this continent, as well as of all the Western Indies. Divine Providence reserved this honour and privilege for the Admiral Don Cristobal Colon, and for no other. For this reason no one can presume to usurp the credit, nor to give it to himself or to another, without wrong, injustice, and injury committed against the Admiral, and consequently without offence against God.

In order that this truth may be made manifest, I will here relate truthfully, and impartially, the information on the subject which I possess. To understand the matter it is necessary to bear in mind that the Admiral left San Lucar, on his third voyage, on the 30th of May 1498, and arrived at the Cape Verde Islands on the 27th of June. He sighted the island of Trinidad on Tuesday, the 31st of July, and soon afterwards, on Wednesday, the 1st of August, he saw the continent to the south of a strait two leagues wide, between it and the island of Trinidad. He called this strait the "mouth of the Serpent", and the mainland, believing it to be an island, he named Isla Sancta. Presently, on the following Friday, he sighted and discovered Paria, which he called Isla de Gracia, thinking that it also was an island. An account of all these discoveries, with a painted outline of the land, was sent by the Admiral to the Sovereigns.

This being understood, we shall now see when Americo Vespucio set out, and with whom, to discover and trade in those parts. Those who may read this history must know that, at that time, Alonso de Hojeda was in Castille, when the account of the discovery and of the form of that land arrived, which was sent by the Admiral to the Sovereigns. This report and map came into the hands of the Bishop Don Juan Rodriguez de Fonseca, afterwards Bishop of Palencia, who had charge of all business connected with the Indies from the beginning, and was then Archdeacon of Seville. The said Alonso de Hojeda was a great favourite of the Bishop, and when the report of the Admiral and the map arrived, Fonseca suggested to Hojeda to go and make more discoveries in the same direction as the Admiral had taken. For when the thread is discovered and placed in the hand, it is an easy matter to reach the skein. Hojeda was aided by the information which the Admiral had collected from the Indians when he served in the first voyage, that there was a continent behind the lands and islands then reached. As he had the favour and goodwill of the Bishop, he looked out for persons who would fit out some ships, for he himself had not sufficient funds. As he was known in Seville as a brave and distinguished man, he found, either there, or perhaps at the port of Santa Maria, whence he sailed, some one who enabled him to fit out four ships. The Sovereigns gave him his commission and instructions, and appointed him captain, for the discovery and purchase of gold and pearls, a fifth being reserved as the royal share, and to treat of peace and friendship with people he should meet with during the expedition.

Thus the first who went to discover after the Admiral was no other than Alonso de Hojeda. Those whom he took, and wanted to take in his company, consisted of the sailors who were acquainted with the voyage to those lands, who were none others but those who had come and gone with the Admiral. Those were the principal mariners of the time. One of them was Juan de la Cosa Biscayan, 143 who went with the Admiral when he discovered this island, and was afterwards with him in the Cuba and Jamaica discovery, the most laborious voyage up to that time. Hojeda also took with him the pilot Bartolomé Roldan, who was well known in this city of San Domingo, and who built, from their foundations, a great number of the houses now standing in the four streets. He too had been with the Admiral in his first voyage, and also in the discovery of Paria and the mainland. Hojeda also took the said Americo, and I do not know whether as pilot, or as a man instructed in navigation and learned in cosmography. For it appears that Hojeda puts him among the pilots he took with him.

I gather from the prologue he addressed to King Rènè of Naples, in the book of his four Navigations, that the said Americo was a merchant, for so he confesses. Probably he contributed some money towards the expenses of fitting-out the four ships, with the condition of receiving a proportionate share of the profits. Although Americo asserts that the King of Castile sent out the expedition, and that they went to discover by his order, this is not true. Three or four, or ten, persons combined, who were possessed of some money, and begged and even importuned the Sovereigns for permission to go and discover and search, with the object of promoting their own profits and interests. Thus Hojeda, owing to his having got possession of the chart which the Admiral had sent home of the mainland he had discovered, for the Sovereigns, and owing to his having with him the pilots and mariners who had been with the Admiral, came to discover the further part of the mainland, which will be described in chapter 166.

It is a thing well known, and established by many witnesses, that Americo went with Alonso de Hojeda, and that Hojeda went after the Admiral had discovered the mainland. It is also proved by Alonso de Hojeda himself. He was produced as a witness in favour of the Crown, when the Admiral Don Diego Colon, next and legitimate successor of the Admiral Don Cristobal Colon, had a lawsuit with the Crown for all the estate of which his father had been dispossessed, as he was by the same cause. Alonso de Hojeda testifies as follows, in his reply to the second question. He was asked "if he knew that the Admiral Don Cristobal Colon had not discovered any part of what is now called mainland, except when he once touched at the part called Paria?" The answer of Hojeda was that the Admiral touched at the island of Trinidad, and passed between that island and the "Boca del Drago", which is Paria, and that he sighted the island of Margarita. Being asked how he knew this, he answered that he knew it because he, the witness, saw the chart which the said Admiral sent to Castille, to the King and Queen our Lords, of what he had discovered at that time: and also because he, the witness, soon afterwards went on his voyage of discovery, and found that the Admiral's account of what he had discovered was the truth. To the fifth question, which refers to what the same Hojeda discovered himself beyond Paria, he replied as follows: "I was the first to go on an exploring expedition after the discovery of the Admiral, and I went first nearly 200 leagues to the south on the mainland, and afterwards came to Paria, going out by the 'Boca del Drago'. There I ascertained that the Admiral had been at the island of Trinidad, bordering on the 'Boca del Drago'." Further on he says: "In the voyage which this witness undertook, he took with him Juan de la Cosa and Americo Vespucio, and other pilots." 144 Alonso de Hojeda says this, among other things, in his deposition and statement.

Two things are thus proved by Hojeda himself. One is that he took Americo with him, and the other that he undertook his voyage to the mainland, after it had been discovered by the Admiral. The latter fact is established beyond any doubt, namely, that the Admiral was the first who discovered Paria, and that he was there before any other Christian whatever was either there or on any other part of the mainland, nor had any tidings of it. The Admiral Don Diego, his son, had proof of this from sixty hearsay witnesses and twenty-five eye-witnesses, as is seen by the records of the lawsuit, which I have not only seen but thoroughly examined. It was also proved that it was owing to the Admiral having first discovered these islands of the Indies, and afterwards Paria, which is the mainland, before anyone else whatever, that the others had the courage to follow his example and become discoverers. It may be held for certain that no one would have undertaken to go on voyages of discovery, and that neither the Indies nor any part of them would have been made known if the Admiral had not led the way. This is proved by sixteen hearsay witnesses, by forty-one who believed it, by twenty who knew it, and by thirteen who gave evidence that in their belief the Admiral made his discoveries before anyone else whatever. Peter Martyr also gives the same testimony in his first Decade, chapters 8 and 9. This author deserves more credit than any of those who have written in Latin, because he was in Castille at the time, and knew all the explorers, and they were glad to tell him all they had seen and discovered, as a man in authority; and because he made his inquiries with a view to writing, as we mentioned in the prologue of the history.

Americo confesses in his first Navigation that he arrived at Paria during his first voyage, saying: "Et provincia ipsa Parias 145 ab ipsis nuncupata est." Afterwards he made the second Navigation, also with Hojeda, as will appear in chapter 162.

Here it is important to note and make clear the error made by the world in general respecting America. What I say is this: As no one had arrived at nor seen Paria before the Admiral, and as the next explorer who arrived was Hojeda, it follows that either Americo was with Hojeda, or came after him. If he was with Hojeda, Hojeda was after the Admiral. The Admiral left San Lucar on the 30th of May, and came in sight of Trinidad and the mainland on the last day of July, and the 1st and 3rd of August, as has been proved. How, therefore, can Americo say, without a perversion of the truth, that he left Cadiz in his first Navigation on the 20th of May of the year of our salvation 1497? The falsehood is clear, and if the statement was made by him in earnest, he committed a great infamy. Even if it is not an intentional falsehood, it seems to be so; for he gives himself an advantage of ten days as regards the Admiral, with reference to the departure from Cadiz, for the Admiral left San Lucar on the 30th of May, and Americo alleges that he departed from Cadiz on the 20th of that month, and also usurps a year, for the Admiral sailed in 1498, while Americo pretends that he set out on his first Navigation in the year 1497. It is true that there would seem to be a mistake, and not an intentional fraud in this, for Americo says that his first Navigation occupied eighteen months, and at the end he asserts that the date of his return to Cadiz was the 15th of October 1499. If he left Cadiz on the 20th of May 1497, the voyage occupied twenty-nine months: seven in the year 1497, all the year 1498, and ten months in the year 1499. It is possible that 1499 may be a misprint for 1498 146 in treating of the return to Castille, and if this was so, there can be no doubt that the fraud was intentional. This fraud or mistake, whichever it may have been, and the power of writing and narrating well and in a good style, as well as Americo's silence respecting the name of his captain, which was Hojeda, and his care to mention no one but himself, and his dedication to King Renè, these things have led foreign writers to name our mainland America, as if Americo alone, and not another with him, had made the discovery before all others. It is manifest what injustice he did if he intentionally usurped what belonged to another, namely, to the Admiral Don Cristobal Colon, and with what good reason this discovery, and all its consequences, should belong to the Admiral, after the goodness and providence of God, which chose him for this work. As it belongs more to him, the said continent ought to be called Columba, after Colon, or Columbo, who discovered it, or else "Sancta" or "De Gracia", the names he himself gave it, and not America after Americo.

Chapter CLXIV.

The Admiral sent five ships 147 with the news of the discovery of the mainland of Paria, and of the pearls. Alonso de Hojeda was then in Spain. I believe myself that he returned at the same time as my uncle, Francisco de Penalosa, knowing that the Admiral had discovered that land and the pearls, and having seen the chart of the new discoveries which the Admiral had sent to the Sovereigns, and that the Admiral said in his letters that it was an island, although he was also inclined to the belief that it was a continent; and being favoured by the Bishop of Badajos, Don Juan de Fonseca, who superintended and managed everything, Hojeda petitioned that he might have licence to discover in those parts either continent, or islands, or whatever he might find. The Bishop gave the licence, signed with his own signature, and not with that of the Sovereign, either because the Sovereigns ordered him to grant such licences, or this one only, which is hard to believe; or because he wished to make the grant of his own authority, and without giving the Sovereigns a share in the matter, the Admiral having complained to the Sovereigns in the year 1495 that it was in opposition to his privileges to give a licence to anyone to undertake discoveries.... I do not see how the Bishop was able to grant the licence in the way he did. But I quite see that as he was a very determined and obstinate man, and was hostile to the Admiral's interests, he may have taken this step actuated by his own audacity, and without consulting the Sovereigns. This is possible, but still I doubt it; for, although he was very intimate with the Sovereigns, this was hardly a thing that he would have dared to do on his own authority. The licence was granted with the limitations that it did not include the territory of the King of Portugal, nor the lands discovered by the Admiral up to the year 1495. Another question arises here: Why was not the land excepted which the Admiral had just discovered, and which was identified by the letters and the chart he had sent to the Sovereigns? To this I cannot give an answer.

That the licence was only signed by the said Bishop, and not by the Sovereigns, there can be no doubt, for Francisco Roldan saw it, and so described it to the Admiral, and I saw Roldan's original letter, as I will presently mention.

Hojeda having obtained the licence, he found persons in Seville who would fit out four caravels or ships, for there were many who were eager to go and discover by means of the thread which the Admiral had put into their hands. For he was the first who opened the gates of that Ocean Sea, which had been closed for so many ages.

Hojeda set out from the port of Santa Maria or of Cadiz in the month of May. If Americo Vespucio does not speak contrary to the truth as regards the day of the month, he does so as regards the year. The date of Hojeda's departure was the 20th of May 1499, not 1497, as Americo says, usurping the honour and glory which belongs to the Admiral, and assuming the whole for himself alone, wishing to give the world to understand that he was the first discoverer of the mainland of Paria, and not the Admiral, to whom is justly and rightfully due all the discovery of all these islands and mainland of the Indies, as has already been proved in chapter 140. In that chapter I endeavoured to leave it doubtful whether Americo had, with intention, tacitly denied that this discovery was made first by the Admiral, and had given the credit of it to himself alone. For I had not then seen what I afterwards gathered from those writings of Americo, and from other writings of those times in my possession, or which I have found. From these I conclude that it was a most false and dishonest thing on the part of Americo to wish to usurp against justice the honour due to the Admiral. The proof of this falsehood is made clear from the evidence of Americo himself, in this way. We will assume what has already been proved in chapter 140, namely:—First, the testimony of such a multitude of witnesses who knew that the Admiral was the first who discovered the mainland of Paria, and consequently no one reached any part of the mainland before him, this being also affirmed by Peter Martyr in the third and ninth chapters of his first Decade; and Hojeda himself, in his deposition, also testified, being unable to deny it, saying that after he had seen the chart in Castille he went to discover, and found that the Admiral had previously arrived at Paria and gone out by the Boca del Drago. Secondly, Americo went with Hojeda, either as a pilot or as one who knew something of the sea, for he is mentioned jointly with Juan de la Cosa and other pilots; or perhaps he went as an adventurer, contributing part of the expenses and having a share in the profits. Thirdly, we refer to what Americo confesses in his first Navigation, which is, that he reached a place called Paria by the Indian natives; also, that in a certain part or province of the coast of the mainland, or in an island where they made war, the Indians wounded twenty-two men and killed one. Now this happened in 1499, as I shall presently prove. What we say is this: The Admiral was the first who discovered the mainland and Paria, Hojeda was the first after the Admiral, and Americo, who went with Hojeda, confesses that they arrived at Paria. The Admiral left San Lucar on the 30th of May 1498; presently, Hojeda and Americo left Cadiz in the following year, 1499. If the Admiral left San Lucar on the 30th of May, and Hojeda and Americo sailed from Cadiz on the 20th of May, and the Admiral departed first, it is clear that the departure of Hojeda and Americo could not have been in that year of 1498, but in the following year of 1499. Even if it can be said that Hojeda and Americo may have departed first on the 20th of May of the same year of 1498 that the Admiral sailed, still the statement of Americo would be false, for he said that he departed in 1497. Now there is no doubt that Hojeda and Americo neither departed in 1497 nor in 1498, but in 1499, and it is, therefore, demonstrated that it was not Americo who first discovered the mainland of Paria, nor anyone else but the Admiral. This is confirmed by what was shown in chapter 140, that Hojeda, in his deposition when he was called as a witness before the Fiscal, said that after he had seen the chart of the land discovered by the Admiral, when he was in Castille, he went on a voyage of discovery himself, and found that the land was as it had been correctly laid down on the chart. Now the Admiral sent this chart with a report to the Sovereigns in the year 1498; on the 18th of October the said ships left Navidad, and my father was on board one of them. Afterwards Hojeda and Americo sailed on the 20th of May, as Americo himself writes, and this can only have been in the following year, 1499. This is confirmed by another reason. The Admiral was informed by the Christians who were in the province of Yaquimo that Hojeda had arrived at the land called Brasil on the 5th of September, and the Admiral wrote to this effect to the Sovereigns by the ships in which the Procurators of the Admiral and of Roldan went home. This was in the year 1499, at the time when Francisco Roldan and his company were about to be, or had been, induced to yield obedience to the Admiral. This was the first voyage that Americo made with Hojeda. It is, therefore, clear that neither Hojeda nor Americo can have left Cadiz in 1497, but they must have sailed in 1499. That this was the first voyage made by Hojeda and Americo in search of the mainland appears from two reasons which have already been mentioned as being given by Americo himself in his first Navigation. One is, that they arrived at a land called by the natives Paria, and the other that the Indians wounded twenty-two men and killed one in a certain island. This latter fact was told to Francisco Roldan by Hojeda's people when the same Roldan went on board the ships of Hojeda. The Admiral sent him as soon as he was informed that Hojeda had reached the land of Brasil. 148

Francisco Roldan wrote to the Admiral from thence these, among other words which I saw in the handwriting of Francisco Roldan, his handwriting being well known to me. The letter begins as follows:—"I make known to your Lordship that I arrived where Hojeda was on Sunday the 29th of September," etc., and he goes on: "this being so, my Lord, I went on board the caravels, and found in them Juan Velasquez and Juan Vizcaino, 149 who showed me a concession made to him for the discovery of new countries, signed by the Lord Bishop, by which he was granted permission to make discoveries in these parts so long as he did not touch the territory of the King of Portugal, nor the territory which had been discovered by your Lordship up to the year 1495. They made discoveries in the land which your Lordship recently discovered. He says that they sailed along the coast for 600 leagues, where they encountered people who fought with them, wounding twenty and killing one. In some places they landed and were received with great honour, and in others the natives would not consent to their landing."

These are the words of Francisco Roldan to the Admiral. Americo, in his first Navigation, says:—"But one of our people was killed and twenty-two wounded, all recovering their health by the help of God." The same Americo also relates that Hojeda and himself arrived at the island Española, as will appear presently. It appears clearly from the evidence of the said Americo, and the agreement of his statement with what his companions told to Francisco Roldan, that they had twenty or twenty-two wounded and one killed, and this was during his first voyage. It also appears from both that they went to and saw Paria, and the coast newly discovered by the Admiral. If this was the first voyage of Americo, and he came to this island in the year 1499, on the 5th of September, having left Cadiz on the 20th of May of the same year, 1499, as has been distinctly shown, it follows that Americo has falsely stated that he left Cadiz in the year 1497. This is also shown by what the Admiral wrote to the Sovereigns when he knew that Hojeda had sailed five months before, in May. He wrote as follows:—"Hojeda arrived at the port where the brasil is, five days ago. These sailors say that as the time is so short since his departure from Castille, he cannot have discovered land, but he may well have got a lading of brasil before it could be prohibited, and as he has done, so may other interlopers." These are the words of the Admiral, and I have seen them in his own handwriting. He intended to explain that little land could have been discovered in five months, and that, if he had not sent Francisco Roldan to prohibit the ships from taking a cargo of brasil, they might easily have done so and have departed, and that the same might be done by any other stranger, unless steps were taken to prevent it.

All these proofs, taken from the letters of the Admiral and of Roldan, cannot be disputed, because they are most certainly authentic, and no doubt can be thrown on any of them. For no one then could tell that this matter would be alleged and brought forward, seeing that during fifty-six or fifty-seven years what was written told a different story, which was the truth, nor was there anything to conceal.

But what Americo has written to make himself famous and give himself credit, tacitly usurping the discovery of the continent which belongs to the Admiral, was done with intention. This is shown by many arguments given in this chapter and in chapter 140. But besides these verbal proofs, I desire to submit others which make the thing most manifest. One is that he inverted the voyages he made, applying the first to the second, and making out that things which belonged to one happened in the other. He asserts that in the first voyage they were absent eighteen months, and this is not possible, for after being absent from Castille for five months they came to this island, and they could not have returned again to the mainland to coast along it for such a distance, owing to contrary winds and currents, except with great difficulty and after a long time. Thus his voyage to the continent only took five months, within which time he arrived here, as has been already explained, and as Hojeda told some of the Spaniards who were here, before he left this island. He then made an inroad on some of the surrounding islands, seizing some of the natives and carrying them off to Castille. According to the statement of Americo, they took 222 slaves, and this occurs at the end of his first Navigation. "And we, following the way to Spain, at length arrived at the port of Cadiz with 222 captured persons," etc. Another statement is that certain injuries and violences done by Hojeda and his followers against the Indians and Spaniards in Xaragua in his first voyage is placed by Americo at the end of his second Navigation. He there says: "We departed, and, for the sake of obtaining many things of which we were in need, we shaped a course for the island of Antiglia, being that which Christopher Columbus discovered a few years ago. Here we took many supplies on board, and remained two months and seventeen days. Here we endured many dangers and troubles from the same Christians who were in this island with Columbus. I believe this was caused by envy, but, to avoid prolixity, I will refrain from recounting what happened." The Portuguese then called this island of Española Antilla, and this Americo used the word Antiglia, because he was writing in Lisbon. In the following chapter I will explain what these troubles from the Spaniards were, and what caused them, which he excuses himself from dwelling upon in order to avoid prolixity. It will then be clearly seen that they happened during his first voyage.

Another point is that they arrived at this island on the 5th of September, as he said, and that they remained, according to him, for two months and two days—that is, all September and October, and two more days of November. He there says that they left this island on the 22nd of July and arrived at the port of Cadiz on the 8th of September. All this is most false. The same may be said of the dates of all the years, months, and days which Americo gives in his Navigations. It thus appears that he designedly wished to take the glory and renown of the discovery of the continent, even keeping silence respecting the name of his own captain, Alonso de Hojeda, and tacitly usurping, as has been said, the honour and glory which belongs to the Admiral for this famous deed, deceiving the world by writing in Latin, and to the King Renè of Naples, there being no one to resist or expose his claim out of Spain, those who then knew the truth being kept in ignorance. I am surprised that Don Hernando Colon, son of the same Admiral, and a person of good judgment and ability, and having in his possession these same Navigations of America, as I know, did not take notice of this injury and usurpation which Americo Vespucio did to his most illustrious father.

Chapter CLXV.

There remains the demonstrations, now proved in detail, of the industrious contrivance of Americo Vespucio, not at first easily conceived, as I believe, but thought out at some subsequent time, by which he attributed to himself the discovery of the greater part of that Indian world, when God had conceded that privilege to the Admiral. Now it is proper to continue the history of what happened to Alonso de Hojeda, with whom Americo went on his first voyage. He departed from the port of Cadiz with four ships, in the month of May. Juan de la Cosa, with all the experience acquired in his voyages with the Admiral, went as pilot, and there were other pilots and persons who had served in the said voyages. Americo also embarked, as has already been mentioned in chap. 140, either as a merchant, or as one versed in cosmography and studies relating to the sea. They sailed in May, according to Americo, but not, as he says, in the year 1497, the true date being 1499, as has already been sufficiently proved. Their course was directed towards the west, to the Canary Islands, then southward. After twenty-seven days 150 (according to the said Americo) they came in sight of land, which they believed to be continental, and they were not deceived. Having come to the nearest land, they anchored at a distance of about a league from the shore, from fear of striking on some sunken rock. They got out the boats, put arms into them, and reached the beach, where they saw an immense number of naked people. They received them with great joy. But the Indians looked on with astonishment, and presently ran away to the nearest forest. The Christians approached them with signs of peace and friendship, but they would not trust the strangers. As the Christians had anchored in an open roadstead, and not in a port, wishing to be out of danger if bad weather came on, they weighed, and stood along the coast to seek for a port, all the shore being crowded with people. After two days they found a good port. (Las Casas then quotes the account of the natives given by Americo Vespucci, respecting which he makes the following comments.) Americo relates all these things in his first Navigation, many of which he could not have known in two, nor three, nor in ten days that he may have been among the Indians, not knowing a single word of their language, as he himself confesses. Such are the statements, that owing to the heat of the sun they move from place to place every eight years; that when the women are enraged with their husbands they create abortions; that they have no rule or order in their marriages; that they have neither king nor lord nor chief in their wars; and others of the same kind. Therefore we can only believe those statements which are based on what he actually saw or might see, such as what the natives ate and drank, that they went naked, that they were of such and such colour, were great swimmers, and other external acts. The rest appears to be all fiction.

Chapter CLXVI.

They left these people and proceeded along the coast, often landing and having intercourse with different tribes, until they arrived at a port where, as they entered, they saw a town built over the water like Venice. Americo says that it contained twenty very large houses, built, like the others he had seen, in the shape of a bell, and raised on very strong piles. At the doors of the houses they had drawbridges, by which, as if they were streets, they went from one house to another. (Las Casas then gives the account of the encounter with the natives of this town on piles, just as it is given by Vespucci.) They made sail from this port, and proceeded for eighty leagues along the coast; and this was the land of Paria discovered by the Admiral, as has already been shown. Here they found another people, with very different customs and language. They anchored and got into their boats to go on shore, where they found over 4,000 natives on the beach. The Indians were so frightened that they did not wait, but fled to the mountains. The Christians having landed, followed a path, and came to many huts, which they believed were those of fishermen. Here they found fish of various kinds, and also one of the iguanas which I have already described, and which astonished them, for they thought it was some very fierce serpent. The bread eaten by these people, says Americo, was made with fish steeped in hot water, and afterwards pounded. From this mass small loaves were kneaded and baked, making very good bread, in his judgment. They found many kinds of fruits and herbs; but they not only took nothing, but left many small things from Castille in the huts, in the hope that thus the fears of the natives would be dispelled, and the Spaniards then returned to the ships. (Las Casas here inserts the account given by Vespucci of a journey inland, and of intercourse with these natives.) Americo then says that the land was populous, and also full of many different animals, few being like those of Spain. He mentions lions, bears, deer, pigs, wild goats, which had a certain deformity, and were unlike ours. But in truth I do not believe that he saw either lions or bears, because lions are very rare, and there cannot have been so many as that he should see them; and the same remark applies to bears. No one who has been to the Indies has even seen goats there, nor can I understand how he can have seen the difference between deer and goats nor how he can have seen pigs, there being none in those parts. Deer he may well have seen, as there are many on the mainland. He says there are no horses, mules, asses, cows, nor sheep, nor dogs, and here he tells the truth, although there is a kind of dog in some parts. He says that there is great abundance of other wild animals of various kinds, but if they were not rabbits he could have little true evidence of having seen them. Of birds of different plumage and species he says that he saw many; and this I believe, for there is an infinite number. He says that the region is pleasant and fertile, full of woods and great forests, which consist of evergreens, yielding fruits of many sorts; and all this is also true.

He then repeats that many people came to see the whiteness and persons of the Spaniards. (I do not know whether he is speaking of this same land, as it would seem, or of another, for he appears to confuse his account here with what he had said before, that they had to depart that night.) He tells us that the natives asked whence the Spaniards came, and they replied that they had come down from heaven to see the things of the earth, which the Indians undoubtedly believed. Here the Christians committed a great sacrilege, thinking to make an agreeable offering to God. As they saw the natives so gentle, meek, and tractable, although neither could understand a single word of what the other said, and therefore the Spaniards could not teach the Indians any doctrine, yet, says Americo, they baptized an infinite number; whence it appears how little Americo, and those who were with him, appreciated the practice of the sacraments and the reverence that is due to them, nor even the disposition and frame of mind with which they should be received. It is manifest that those Christians, in baptizing the natives, committed a great offence against God. Americo says that after they were baptized, the Indians used the word charaybi, which means that they called the Spaniards men of great knowledge. This statement is a thing to laugh at, for the Spaniards did not even know the Indian names for bread or for water, which are among the first that we learn in acquiring a language; yet during the few days they remained Americo wants us to believe that he understood that charaybi signifies men of great knowledge. Here Americo declares that the natives called this land Paria; and he conceals, what he must have known, that the Admiral had already been there several days, which was a reason for not remaining silent.

Chapter CLXVII.

They decided upon leaving this port and the sweetwater gulf formed by the island of Trinidad and the mainland of Paria by the "Boca del Drago", and I suspect that, as this was a place which was notoriously discovered by the Admiral, Americo kept silence as to the name of "Boca del Drago" intentionally. For it is certain that Hojeda and Americo were within this port, because the same Hojeda gave evidence to that effect on oath, as well as many other witnesses also on oath, as is affirmed in the evidence taken by the Fiscal. Here Americo says that the voyage had now lasted thirteen months, but I do not believe it. Even if he tells the truth as regards the number of months, this must have been in the second voyage, which he afterwards made with the same Hojeda, as I think must be understood, and not in this first voyage, as is shown, for many reasons already set forth, and for others which will hereafter be given. Finally departing from Paria, they proceeded along the coast and arrived at Margarita, an island sighted by the Admiral and named by him Margarita, although he did not stop there. Hojeda landed and walked over part of it, as he himself says, and those same witnesses who were with them also say that he arrived there, though they neither deny nor affirm that he landed; but there need be no doubt of it, for it is a pleasant island. This, however, little affects the question. It may be believed that they here bartered for pearls, although he does not say so, for other discoverers who came after him traded at the island of Margarita. Hojeda extended his journey to the province and gulf called Cuquibacoa in the language of the Indians, which is now named Venezuela in our language, and thence to Cabo de la Vela, where they now fish for pearls. He gave it that name of Cabo de la Vela, which it still retains; and a row of islands running east and west was discovered, some of which were called the Islands of the Giants.

Thus had Hojeda coasted the mainland for 400 leagues, 200 to the east of Paria, where he sighted the first land, and this was the only land that he and those with him discovered. Paria and Margarita were discovered by the Admiral, as well as a great part of the said 200 leagues from Margarita to Cabo de la Vela, for the Admiral saw the chain of mountains to the westward as he sailed along, so that all this discovery is due to him. For it does not follow that, in order to be the discoverer of a land or island, a navigator must have passed along the whole of it. For instance, it is clear that the island of Cuba was personally discovered by the Admiral, and for this it is not necessary that he should have gone into every corner of it; and the same remark applies to Española and the other islands, and also to the mainland, however large it may be, and however far it may extend, the Admiral discovered it. From this it appears that Americo exaggerated when he said that in his first Navigation they sailed along the coast for 860 leagues. This is not true, as is proved by the confession of Hojeda, a man who had no desire to lose anything of his own glory and rights, for he said, as appeared in chapter 140, that he discovered 200 leagues beyond Paria, and the coast from Paria to Cuquibacoa, which is now Venezuela. I have added as far as Cabo de la Vela, because I found it so deposed in the process by several witnesses who afterwards knew all that land well, had intercourse with the discoverers, and went with them in their voyages of discovery, though not in that voyage of Hojeda; but the testimony was given when the events were recent, and consequently well known. Hojeda himself did not mention Cabo de la Vela, because it is near the Gulf of Venezuela, and is all one land; and of the gulf and province he made principal mention, as a thing notable and important, and called by the natives Cuquibacoa.

Along all this land or sea-coast traversed by Hojeda, Americo, and his company, they got gold and pearls by barter and exchange, but the quantity is not known, nor the deeds they perpetrated in the land. Having left Margarita, they went to Cumanà and Maracapana, which are respectively seven and twenty leagues from Margarita. There are people on the sea-shore, and before reaching Cumanà there is a gulf where the water of the sea forms a great angle extending fourteen leagues into the land, round which there are numerous and populous tribes. The first, nearly at the mouth of the bay, is Cumanà. A large river falls into the sea near the village, in which there are numbers of the creatures we call lagartos, but they are nothing more than the crocodiles of the river Nile. As they were under the necessity of refitting the ships, they being defective for so long a voyage as a return to Spain, and also being in want of provisions, they arrived at a port which Americo calls the best in the world. But he does not say where it was, nor does he mention Hojeda. According to what I remember forty-three years after having been there, and over fifty years since the voyage of Hojeda, I suspect that it must be a gulf called Cariaco, which runs fourteen leagues into the land, the entrance being seven leagues from Margarita, on the mainland near Cumanà. Further, it occurs to me that I heard that at that time Hojeda entered and repaired his ships, and built a brigantine in the port called Maracapana, but this, though a port, is not the best in the world.

At last they left the port, wherever it may have been, within those 200 leagues of mainland from Paria onwards. They were received and served by the people of that region, who were innumerable, according to Americo, as if they had been angels from heaven, and as Abraham had known the three, so they were recognised as angels. They unloaded the ships and brought them to land, always helped by the labour of the Indians. They careened and cleared them, and built a new brigantine. They say that during all the time that they were there, which was thirty-seven days, they never had any need of touching their Castillian provisions, because they were supplied with deer, fish, native bread, and other food; and if they had not been so provided, says Americo, they would have been in great distress for provisions in returning to Spain. During all the time they were there they went on shore among the villages, in which they were received with hospitality, honour, and festivity. This is certain (as will be seen further on in the course of the history, if it please the all-powerful God), that all these people of the Indies, being by nature most simple and kind, know well how to serve and please those who come to them, when they look upon them as friends. When after having repaired their ships and built the brigantine they determined to return to Spain, Americo here says that their hosts made great complaints of another cruel and ferocious tribe, inhabiting an island at a distance of 100 leagues; saying that they came at a certain time of the year over the sea, to make war, and that they carried off their captives, killing and eating them. They showed their grief with so much feeling and persistency, says Americo, that it moved us to compassion, and we offered to avenge them. This made them rejoice greatly, says Americo, and they said they would like to go also. But the Christians, for many reasons, would only consent that seven natives should accompany them, on condition that they should not be taken back to their country in the ships, but that they should return in their own canoes, and to this, he says, both parties consented. I do not know what interpreter made these agreements, nor who understood all that was said, but it is obvious that they could not have known the language in thirty-seven days. And how could Hojeda and Americo, and those of their company, know whether the islanders had just cause for war or not? Were these men so certain of the justice of the natives that, without further delay, merely because they made complaints, they offered to avenge them? Pray God that they did not make this war to fill up their ships with natives, with a view to selling them for slaves, as they afterwards did in Cadiz; work too often done by our people against these unfortunate tribes and lands. They set out, and after seven days they came upon numerous islands, some peopled and others uninhabited, says Americo, at last arriving at their destination. These islands cannot be others than those we reach in coming from Spain, such as Dominica and Guadalupe, and the others that lie in that line. Presently they saw, he says, a great crowd of people, who, when they saw the ships and the boats approaching the shore well armed with guns, sent a body of 400 to the water's edge, with many women, naked and armed with bows and arrows and shields, and all painted in different colours, and adorned with wings and feathers of large birds, so that they appeared very warlike and fierce. When the boats had approached to the distance of a cross-bow shot, they advanced into the water, and discharged a great number of arrows to prevent their advance. The Christians discharged the firearms and killed many of them, and fearing the discharge and the firing, they left the water and came on shore. A body of forty-two men then landed from the boats and attacked them. The natives did not fly, but stood their ground manfully, and fought valiantly like lions, defending themselves and their country. They fought for two long hours, first with their guns and cross-bows, and afterwards with their swords and lances, killing many; and that they might not all perish, those of the natives who were able, fled into the woods. Thus the Christians remained victorious, and they returned to their ships with great joy at having sent so many people to hell who had never offended them. On another day, in the morning, they saw a great multitude of natives, making the air resound with horns and trumpets, painted and armed for a second battle.

The Christians determined to send fifty-seven men against them, divided into four companies, each with a captain, intending, says Americo, to make friends with them if possible, but if not, to treat them as enemies, and to make slaves of as many as they could take. This is said by Americo, and it is to be noted here how he makes a pretext of truth and justice and legality, when the Spaniards had promised to go a hundred leagues on a message of war and vengeance. Yet they would come to treat of friendship with the natives, seeking occasion to gratify their covetousness, which was what they came for from Castille. Such are the pretexts and unworthy artifices that have always been used for the destruction of these natives.

They went on shore, but the Indians, owing to the fire from the guns, did not venture to oppose their landing, yet they awaited them with great steadiness. The naked men fought against the clothed men with great valour for a long time, but the clothed made a fearful slaughter among the naked men, the swords taking great effect on their naked bodies. The survivors fled when they saw that they were being cut to pieces. The Christians pursued them to a village, capturing all they could, to the number of twenty-five. They returned with their victory, but with the loss of one killed and twenty-two wounded. They then sent away the seven natives who had come with them from the mainland. They departed, says Americo, taking with them as prisoners seven natives given to them by the Spaniards, three men and four women, as their captives, and they were very joyful, admiring that deed performed by the forces of the Christians. All this is related by Americo, who adds that they returned to Spain and arrived at Cadiz with 222 Indian captives, where they were, according to him, very joyfully received, and where they sold all the slaves. Who will now ask whence they stole and carried off the 200 natives? This, as other things, is passed over in silence by Americo. It should be noted here by readers who know something of what belongs to right and natural justice, that although these natives are without faith, yet those with whom Americo went had neither just cause nor right to make war on the natives of those islands and to carry them off as slaves, without having received any injury from them, nor the slightest offence. Moreover, they were ignorant whether the accusations of those of the mainland against the islanders were just or unjust. What report, or what love would be spread about and sown among the natives, touching those Christians, when they left them wounded and desolate? But we must proceed, for, touching this matter, grandis restat nobis via.

Chapter CLXVIII.

Here Americo is convicted of a palpable falsehood, for he says that he went to Castille from that island where he perpetrated such atrocities, making no mention of having first gone to Española, as he did. He refers the visit to Española to his second voyage, but this is not true, as has already been proved in chap. 162. It is not the fact that they went to Castille from the island where they made war and ill-treated the people: as can be proved from the witnesses examined before the Royal Fiscal, in the lawsuit between Don Diego Colon and the King respecting the granting and observance of his privileges, of which I have often made mention before. They deposed that Alonso de Hojeda, with whom Americo sailed in his first voyage, went along the coast to Cuquibacoa, which is Venezuela, and the Cabo de la Vela, and that thence they went to Española. Thus a witness named Andres de Morales made oath, whom I knew well, a principal pilot and a veteran of these Indies, citizen of Santo Domingo. He said in his deposition, in answer to the fifth question, as follows: "that he knew what happened during that voyage." Asked how he knew, he said: "that he knew because he had often been with Juan de la Cosa and with Alonso de Hojeda, and talked over this voyage, and that they went from the island of Roquemes in the Canaries, and arrived at the mainland near the province of Paria, passing on to the island of Margarita, thence to Maracapana, discovering the coast as far as the Cacique Ayarayte, and thence, from port to port, to the Island of the Giants, the province of Cuquibacoa, and the Cabo de la Vela, which name was given to it by the said Hojeda and Juan de la Cosa, and thence they went to the island of Española." These are his words. Now they could not go from a place so far to leeward, to the island where they committed their depredations, because it must have been one of those towards the east, such as Guadalupe, and the islands near it. It would be very difficult to work to windward against wind and current, which are continuous. This is confirmed by the fact that they reached Brazil in Española, which is the port of Yaquimo, 151 and the proper and natural landfall from Cabo de la Vela. If they had repaired the ships and taken in provisions in that port of the mainland, how was it that it was found necessary to repair and take in provisions again at Española? How was it that the witnesses, and especially the pilot, Andres de Morales, who seems to intimate that he went with them, do not mention that Hojeda had built a brigantine and repaired his ships in some port of the mainland, that being a remarkable event. It would strengthen the veracity of his statements with reference to the discovery of that mainland having been made by him, which was the object of the suit presided over by the Fiscal against the Admiral. It is clear that Americo transferred things which happened in the first voyage to the second, while events of the second are referred to the first voyage, as we have demonstrated already in chap. 142, being silent respecting many things, and adding others which never happened. For example, the building of the brigantine and repairing of the ships on the mainland certainly happened, and I know that it was so, being notorious at that time; but it was during the second voyage, and not the first; while the coming to the island Española, where certain scandals were caused by Hojeda, to which I shall presently refer, took place in the first voyage, and not in the second, as Americo represents. I further say that Hojeda never came to discover, trade, or settle on the mainland, without visiting Española. But his coming in the first voyage is denied or concealed by Americo by silence. From the time that Hojeda left Spain until he arrived at Española there was an interval of five months, which does not leave time for all that he is said to have done during that first voyage.

Returning to the first voyage of Hojeda, with whom Americo went by the correct route, and not by the interpolated and confused way alleged by Americo, we say that from the province of Cuquibacoa, now called Venezuela, and the Cabo de la Vela, he came to this island of Española, and anchored on the 5th of September, as I have already said in chap. 164, at Brazil, which is in the province of Yaquimo, 152 and I even believe further down, near that which is now called Cabana, the land and dominion of a king named Haniguayabá. The Spaniards, who were in that province of Yaquimo, presently knew of the arrival, either from the Indians, or because they saw the vessels come in from the sea. They knew that it was Hojeda, and word was presently sent to the Admiral, who was at San Domingo, having recently made peace with Roldan and his companions. The Admiral ordered two or three caravels to be got ready, and sent Roldan with a force to prohibit the cutting of brasil wood, suspecting that Hojeda would load with it. Roldan was also ordered to prevent the newcomer from doing any other mischief, as Hojeda was known to be most audacious in doing what he chose, it being a word and a deed with him, as they say. Roldan arrived at the port of Yaquimo, or near it, with his caravels, and landed on the 29th of that month of September. He then learnt from the Indians that Hojeda was close by. Roldan, with twenty-six of his men, came within a league and a half, and sent five men by night, as spies, to see what force was with Hojeda. They found that he was coming to reconnoitre Roldan, for the Indians had told him that Roldan had arrived with a large force in three caravels. Roldan was known and feared in all that land, and the natives told Hojeda that Roldan had sent for him to come where he was; but this was not the case. Hojeda only had fifteen men with him, having left the rest in his four ships, which were in a port at a distance of eight leagues. He had come to get bread in the village of the cacique Haniguayabá, and they were making it, not venturing to do anything else, fearing that Roldan would come to seize them. Hojeda, with five or six men, came to where Roldan was, and entered into general conversation, Roldan inquiring how Hojeda had come to that island, and especially to that part of it, without leave from the Admiral, and why he had not first gone to where the Admiral was. Hojeda answered that he was on a voyage of discovery, and that he was in great need of provisions and his ships of repairs, so that he had no other alternative, and that he could not reach any nearer place. Roldan then asked him by what right he was making discoveries, and whether he had a royal licence that he could show to entitle him to get supplies without asking the permission of the governor. He answered that he had such a licence, but that it was on board his ship, eight leagues distant. Roldan said that it must be shown to him, otherwise he would be unable to give an account to the Admiral concerning the business on which he had been sent. Hojeda complied as far as he was able, saying that when he was despatched from that port he would go to make his reverence to the Admiral, and to tell him many things, some of which he mentioned to Roldan. These were, I have no doubt, the questions then spoken of at Court, touching the deprivation of the Admiral, for, as Roldan wrote, they were things which were not fit to be discussed in letters.

Roldan left Hojeda there and went with his caravels to the place where the caravels of Hojeda were at anchor, and found some persons on board who had been in Española with the Admiral, and had served with him in the discovery of Paria, having returned in the five ships, especially one Juan Velasquez and Juan Vizcaino, 153 who showed him the concession signed by the Bishop Don Juan de Fonseca, which I have already mentioned in chap. 164. They informed him of the events of the voyage, and how much of the mainland they had discovered, and how they had lost one man killed, and twenty or more wounded, in a fight, as was stated in the said chap. 164, in which it is proved that this happened during the first voyage of Hojeda. Francisco Roldan also learnt from them that they had found gold, and brought it in the form of guaninas, which are certain trinkets, well and artificially worked, such as they know how to make in Castille, but the gold was below the standard. They brought antlers, and said they had seen deer, rabbits, and the skin of a tiger cat; also a collar made of the nails of animals, all which was news to those who lived in Española. Roldan, knowing this, and believing that Hojeda would do what he had promised; that is, that when he had got his supply of bread in that village he would go to the port of San Domingo to visit the Admiral by land, ordered the caravels to do what they had to do, and I believe this was to get a cargo of brasil wood. Roldan went from Yaquimo to Xaragua, a distance of eighteen leagues, and visited the Christians who were allotted to the villages of the Indians, doing what seemed best to him, and then returned to report the things that had been said to him by Hojeda to the Admiral, which could not have been the best news in the world; for when the five ships came with intelligence of the rebellion of Roldan, they discussed at court the deposition of the Admiral, a thing which Hojeda would not be the last to know, being favoured by the Bishop Don Juan de Fonseca, and neither being friendly to the Admiral and his affairs. As regards the Bishop this was quite notorious, and I saw it with my eyes, felt it with my feeling, and understood it with my understanding. As to Hojeda, it appeared afterwards that he must have left Española, discontented with the Admiral.

Chapter CLXIX.

Roldan took leave of Hojeda, believing that everything that glittered was gold, and Hojeda, having got the bread about which he had arranged, instead of taking the road to Santo Domingo to see the Admiral, and give an account to him of what he had done during his voyage, as he had promised to Roldan, and to report the news from Castille, went with his four ships towards the west, in the direction of the gulf and port of Xaragua. The Christians who were living there, in the villages of the Caciques, received him with joy, and gave him and his people all they needed, although not from the sweat of their own brows, but from that of the Indians, for of the latter the

78

Spaniards are accustomed to be very liberal. As one of their caravels was very unseaworthy, and could no longer be kept above water, they made the Indians work, and they gave much help until she was repaired, assisting in every other way that was needed. While he was there he found that there were people who regretted the free life they had been so recently leading under Roldan, who were ill-disposed towards the affairs of the Admiral, and who were discontented because they could not now do as they pleased. One of their most common complaints was that their wages were not paid. Hojeda, moved either by the disposition he found in these people, or by the expectation of profit for himself, began to encourage the discontent, saying that he would join with them, and, uniting them with his own people, that he would go to the Admiral and demand payment in the name of the Sovereigns, and force him to pay, even if he did so unwillingly. He declared that he had powers from the Sovereigns to do this, and that he and Alonso de Carvajal had received them, when the Admiral returned in the year 1498, that they might come and constrain him to make the payments. He added many other arguments, according to what they said, in great prejudice of the Admiral, and to excite the people against him, to which the greater part inclined, being unprincipled men, friends of turbulence and unrest, and without fear either of God or of the mischief that would follow in that island, both to Christians and Indians.

There were some, however, who did not wish to join in the foolish and evil deeds of Hojeda. These were in a certain farm or village near Xaragua. For all were scattered among the Indian villages, to be fed and maintained by the natives, which could not be done if they all remained together. As these men refused their approval when they were incited, either by letters or by word of mouth, or because they had among them some one who was obnoxious to Hojeda in times past, he arranged one night, in concert with those who had joined him, to attack the loyal men and wreak his vengeance on them, or do them some other injury; and this was done, with the result that several men were killed and wounded on both sides.

This caused great scandal in the land, among Indians as well as Christians, so that disturbances even worse than those of Roldan, recently appeased, would have arisen if God, using the same Roldan as His instrument, had not obviated the danger. Roldan now returned from Santo Domingo to Xaragua. Either because the Admiral suspected that Hojeda would return and cause injury, both to Christians and Indians, and wished to be certain that he had left the island; or because he had received intelligence from the Christians who remained loyal of what was taking place, for they sent messages by Indians every eight days, he finally despatched Roldan to Xaragua, who heard on the road of the scandals and mischief done by Hojeda, and of the object he announced. Roldan then sent to one Diego de Escobar, a leading man among those who had always followed him, ordering him to collect as large a force as possible from among those who had not been influenced by Hojeda, and to come with them to Xaragua. He collected all he could from the villages in which the Christians were scattered, and both arrived at Xaragua on two successive days. Hojeda had by that time returned to his ships.

Francisco Roldan wrote a letter to Hojeda, pointing out the scandals, deaths, and mischief he had caused, the disservice that the Sovereigns would receive from such conduct, the disturbance caused in the colony, the good will which the Admiral entertained towards him, and urging him not to adopt a course which would cause loss to all. In order that the evils might be forgotten, as what was done could not be helped, he proposed that Hojeda should at least come and excuse himself. Hojeda would not place himself in such peril, for he knew Roldan to be an astute and resolute man, and with no small intelligence. Roldan then sent Diego de Escobar to confer with Hojeda, who was not less able than the other two. I knew him well during many years. Escobar set before Hojeda the heinous character of what he had done as strongly as he could, and urged him to come to Roldan. Hojeda replied that it was what he wished to do. Escobar returned without having been able to make a definite arrangement. But Roldan, believing that Hojeda would agree, sent one Diego de Truxillo, who, as soon as he came on board the ship, was seized and put in irons. Hojeda then landed and marched to Xaragua with twenty armed men. He found there one Toribio de Linares, whom I also knew well. He was seized and taken to the ships, where he was put in irons. These proceedings were reported by the Indians to Roldan, who was then at a distance of a league from Xaragua. Roldan quickly set out in pursuit with the men he had with him, well equipped, but Hojeda was already out of his reach. He then sent one Hernando de Estepa, whom I also knew well, to whom Hojeda said that unless one Juan Pintor, who had left the ship, was given up (a man whom I also knew, and who only had one hand), he swore he would hang the two prisoners he had in irons. What harm had these done to merit hanging, because Juan Pintor had deserted! Hojeda got under weigh with his ships, and proceeded along the coast to some villages and a province called Cahay, where there is a charming country and people, ten or twelve leagues from Xaragua. Here he landed with forty men, and seized all the provisions he wanted by force, especially yams and sweet potatoes, for here are the best and finest in the island, leaving both Christians and Indians in great want. Seeing that he had made sail, Roldan sent Diego de Escobar along the sea-shore in pursuit with twenty-five men. But as they arrived at night, Hojeda had already returned to his ships. Soon afterwards, Roldan followed in pursuit with twenty men, and, having arrived at Cahay, he found there a letter which Hojeda had written to Diego de Escobar, declaring that he would hang his two prisoners if his man, Juan Pintor, was not restored. Roldan then ordered Diego de Escobar to get into a canoe, manned, as the sailors say, by Indian rowers, and to go within hail of the ships. He was to tell Hojeda, on the part of Roldan, that as he would not trust him and come to speak with him, he was willing to come to the ships, trusting in his honour, and asking that he would send a boat with this object. Hojeda perceived that his game was now made; but another thought occurred to him, which was that Francisco Roldan had brought his drums on his back, as the saying is. Hojeda sent a very good boat, for he had only one such, with eight very valiant seamen, with their lances, swords, and shields. Coming within a stone's-throw of the beach, they called out that Roldan should embark. Roldan asked, "How many did the captain say were to come with me." They answered, "Five or six men." Roldan presently ordered that Diego de Escobar should get in first, then Pero Bello, Montoya, and Hernan Brabo, and Bolaños. They would not consent that any more should get into the boat. Then Roldan said to one Pedro de Illanes that he must take him to the boat on his back, and as he wanted some one else at his side, he took another man named Salvador. Having all got into the boat, Roldan dissimulated, saying to those who were rowing that they should row towards the land. They did not wish to do so. He and his men put their hands to their swords, and laid about them with such effect that some were killed, others jumped overboard, and all were made prisoners, as well as an Indian archer kidnapped from the islands, only one escaping by swimming. They were brought on shore, and thus Hojeda was left without his best boat, of which he had much need, and also without quite so much pride and insolence. Hojeda, seeing that his artifice had failed, and his intentions were frustrated, resolved to resume the negotiation with more humility. So he got into a small boat with Juan de la Cosa, his principal pilot, a gunner, and four more, and pulled towards the shore. Francisco Roldan, knowing him to be reckless and valiant, and even thinking that he might venture to attack, got ready the large boat with seven rowers and fifteen fighting men, and a good canoe capable of holding fifteen more, all "à pique", as the sailors say. Being on the water, as soon as they were within hailing distance, Hojeda said that he wished to speak with Francisco Roldan. Coming nearer, Francisco Roldan asked him why he had perpetrated those scandalous and culpable acts. He replied that it was because they told him that the Admiral had given orders to apprehend him. Roldan assured him that it was false, and that the Admiral had no intention of doing him harm, but rather to help him and do him honour, and that if he would come to Santo Domingo he would find this to be true by his own experience. Finally Hojeda asked that his boat and men might be restored, no longer caring about Juan Pintor, representing that he could not return to Spain without his boat. Francisco Roldan saw the difficulty in which Hojeda was placed—for there had been a terrible gale just before, and Hojeda's largest ship had dragged her anchors, and had been driven more than two cross-bow shots nearer the shore, where there was danger of ship and crew being lost; also because if Hojeda remained on the island there would be greater confusion caused by him than had previously been caused by Roldan himself. For these reasons Roldan decided to restore the boat with the men, if Hojeda would restore the two prisoners he had seized and ill-treated. This was arranged. He departed to make an incursion, which he said he had to make, and according to what a clergyman who was with him said, and two or three other honest men who were left, the raid that he sought to make was what he intended to do against the person and affairs of the Admiral, and I firmly believe that he had means of knowing that the Sovereigns were considering the removal of the Admiral from his place. For Hojeda was in favour with the Bishop Fonseca, and, on the other hand, the same Bishop always viewed the Admiral with disfavour, justly or unjustly, as to men I say, "God knows."

According to what I suspect, when Hojeda left Española he went to load his ships with Indians, either in some part of that island, or in the Island of San Juan, 154 or in some of the neighbouring islands, for he brought to Spain and sold at Cadiz 222 slaves, as Americo confessed in his first Navigation. This, with the other injuries and outrages perpetrated on Christians and Indians by Hojeda, was his cargo. From what has been seen in this chapter, the falsehoods of Americo are apparent, and the tyrannies committed in this his first voyage, when he accompanied Hojeda, as well as the way in which he confused the events of the two voyages, are now made as evident as that the sun shines. Americo says, respecting the scandals of Hojeda which took place during the first voyage, but which he places in the second, as follows:

"We departed, and, for the sake of obtaining many things of which we were in need, we shaped a course for the island of Antiglia, being that which Christopher Columbus discovered a few years ago. Here we took many supplies on board, and remained two months and 17 days. Here we endured many dangers and troubles from the same Christians who were in this island with Columbus. I believe this was caused by envy; but to avoid prolixity I will refrain from recounting what happened. We departed from the said island on the 22nd of July."

All this is false. He says that he does not describe the troubles they suffered, to avoid prolixity, giving to understand that they suffered unjustly; and he does not tell the cause, or what were the outrages that they committed. Moreover, to place these scandals in the second voyage is also false, as has already been sufficiently shown. To state that the date of departure was the 22nd of July is still more false. For that date was almost at the end of February in the year 1500, and I even believe in March, as appears from the letters which I saw and had in my possession. I know the handwriting of Francisco Roldan, who wrote every eight or fifteen days to the Admiral, when he went to watch Hojeda. The fact is that the date which should belong to the second he put in the first voyage; and the outrages and harm those who were with him did in the first, he referred to as injuries done to them, without provocation, in the second voyage.

Evidence of Witnesses (In the Lawsuit) Respecting the Voyage of Pinzon and Solis.

Antonio Garcia, a pilot, saw the drawing of what had been discovered by Juan Diaz, and it is all one coast. 155

Vicente Yañez Pinson deposed that this witness and Juan de Solis went by order of their Highnesses, and discovered all the land that up to this time has been discovered from the island of Guanaja to the province of Camarona, following the coast towards the east as far as the provinces of Chabaca and Pintigron, which were discovered by this witness and Juan de Solis, who likewise discovered, in following along the coast, a great bay to which they gave the name of the Bay of the Nativity. Thence this witness discovered the mountains of Caria, 156 and other land further on. 157

Rodrigo de Bastidas said that Yañez and Juan Diaz de Solis went to discover below Veragua. He did not know how much they discovered, but it is all one coast with that which was first discovered by the Admiral.

Nicolas Perez said that the Admiral, in that voyage when he went to Veragua, discovered Cape Gracias a Dios, and that all beyond that is discovered, was discovered by Yañez and Juan Diaz de Solis; that this appears by the seachart drawn by them, and that by it all who go to those parts are guided.

Pedro de Ledesma, 158 pilot, said that he went in company of Vicente Yañez and Juan Solis by order of their Highnesses, and saw what Vicente Yañez and Juan de Solis discovered beyond the land of Veragua, in a part towards the north, 159 all that which has been made known up to the present time, from the island of Guanaja towards the north; and that these lands are called Chabaca and Pintigron, and that they reached in a northerly direction as far as 23½ degrees, and that in this part the said Don Cristobal Colon neither went, nor discovered, nor saw.

Las Casas on The Voyage of Pinzon and Solis.

160

After the Admiral left the solitude and the hardships he suffered in Jamaica and came to Castille, it being known what he had discovered, there presently agreed together one Juan Diaz de Solis and Vicente Yañez Pinzon (brother of Martin A. Pinzon, of whom we said that he helped the Admiral to fit out in the town of Palos, and went with him, taking Vicente Yañez and another brother, when he sailed on the first voyage to discover these Indies, as has been explained in the first book) to set out and discover, and to continue the route which the Admiral had left on his fourth and last voyage of discovery. These went to take up the thread from the island or islands of Guanajes, which we said that the Admiral had discovered in his last voyage, and they turned to the east. 161

These two discoverers sailed 162 (as may be gathered from the statement of witnesses called by the Fiscal in the lawsuit with the second Admiral) towards the west from the Guanajes, and must have arrived near the Golfo Dolce, although they did not see it because it is concealed, but they saw the openings made by the sea into the land, which contains the Golfo Dolce and that of Yucatan, and it is like a great gulf or bay. (The mariners give the name of bay to the sea that is between two lands in the form of an open port, which would be a port if it was not that it is very large, but being very capacious and not closed, they call it a bay, the i and a in bahia being pronounced separately.) Thus, as they saw that great angle made by the sea between the two lands, the one which is on the left hand having its back to the east, and this is the coast which contains the port of Caballos and in front of it the Golfo Dolce, and the other on the right hand, which is the coast of the province of Yucatan. It appeared to them to be a great bay, and Vicente Yañez, therefore (in the sworn deposition he made in the said lawsuit, when he was called a witness by the Fiscal), said that, sailing from the island of Guanajes, the coast stretching along, they discovered a great bay to which they gave the name of the "Great Bay of the Nativity", and thence they discovered the hills of Caria, 163 and other lands further on. According to the other witnesses, they then turned north. 164 From all this it appears certain that they then discovered a great part of the kingdom of Yucatan, but as afterwards there was no one who would continue that discovery, nothing more was known of the edifices of that kingdom, whence the territory and grandeur of the kingdoms of New Spain might easily have been discovered. But they were found by chance from the island of Cuba, as, please God, will be set forth in Book III of this history.

And it must here be remarked that these discoverers were chiefly actuated in their enterprize by emulation of the Admiral, and of what he had discovered before, in the service of the Sovereigns. As if the Admiral had not been the first to open the gates of the ocean which had been closed for so many thousands of ages before, and had not shown the light by which all might see how to discover. The Royal Fiscal devoted all his studies to prove that the parts of the mainland discovered by the other explorers were distinct from those which the Admiral had discovered, and he would make a point that the mainland was not so long; his object being to diminish the Admiral's credit, and to make out that the Sovereigns were less obliged to recognise the inestimable services he had performed, and to fulfil the promises they had made, and by which they were bound so justly and with such good reason. This was a great injustice.

With reference to this design, the Fiscal put the question whether the witnesses knew that the discoveries made by others were distinct from those made by the Admiral. For the most part he got the answers he wanted from the sailors, who said it was a different land. But they were not asked if it was all one mainland, nor did they deny that. But others, especially two honourable men whom I knew well, the one Rodrigo de Bastidas, of whom we have already treated, the other a pilot named Andres de Morales, understanding the injury that the prosecutor was trying to do the Admiral, deposed many times, on different occasions in the course of the lawsuit, that the lands others had discovered were to the west of those discovered by the Admiral, but that the whole was one continuous land. True that Vicente Yañez and Juan de Solis went to discover beyond Veragua, along that coast, but all the land that they or any others discovered of the region called the main was all one coast, and continuous with what the Admiral discovered first. Others, besides these two, say it is all one coast from Paria, though provinces have different names, and there are also different languages. This was then declared by witnesses who had been there, and knew it well by having used their own eyes, and now it would be needless to seek further for witnesses than in the grocers' shops in Seville. Thus it cannot be denied to the Admiral, except with great injustice, that as he was the first discoverer of those Indies, so he was also of the whole of our mainland, and to him is due the credit, by discovering the province of Paria, which is a part of all that land. For it was he that put the thread into the hands of the rest, by which they found the clew to more distant parts. Consequently, his rights ought most justly to be complied with and respected throughout all that land, even if the region was still more extensive, just as they should be respected in Española and the other islands. For it was not necessary for him to go to every part, any more than it is necessary in taking possession of an estate, as the jurists hold.

Notes

1. Amerigo Vespucci, son caractère, ses écrits (même les moins authentiques), sa vie, et ses navigations. Par F. A. de Varnhagen, Ministre du Brazil en Perou. (Lima, 1865.)

2. Vita e lettere d'Amerigo Vespucci, Gentiluomo Florentino, raccolte ed illustrate dall' Abate Angelo Maria Bandini. (4to, Firenze, 1745.)

3. Viaggi d'Amerigo Vespucci con la vita, l'elogio, e la dissertazione justicativa di questo celebre navigatore, del Padre Stanislao Canovai, delle scuole pie, pubblico professore di Matematico. Opera postuma. (Firenze, 8vo, 1817.)

4. The first of these letters was published by Bandini from a manuscript found in the Riccardi Library at Florence. It is intended to describe the voyage with Hojeda in 1499. The second appeared in the edition of Marco Polo by Baldelli in 1827, and was also found in the Riccardi Library. It describes an imaginary voyage to the East Indies. The third describes a Portuguese voyage, and was published by Bartolozzi in 1789. It was discovered in the archives of the old Secretariat of State at Florence, among papers which belonged to the Strozzi Library. All three profess to be addressed to Lorenzo di Medici.

They are reprinted by Varnhagen, pp. 69-86.

5. Bandini, Vita, xxiv.

6. There are sixty-eight letters to him, 1483-91, chiefly on business matters.

7. Nav., iii, 316.

8. Four sailed for Española, under the command of Aguado, on 5th August 1495. Others were probably used for the voyage of Pero Alonzo Niño, which sailed on June 15th, 1496; and for the third expedition of Columbus in 1498.

9. On the authority of Muñoz, quoted by Navarrete (iii, 317 n.). More recent researches have failed to discover these entries seen by Muñoz in the second book of Gastos de las armadas de las Indias of the "Casa de Contratacion"; and Mr. Harrisse, therefore, assumes that they never existed. This does not follow, and the evidence of so high an authority as Muñoz cannot so lightly be set aside. It is true, however, that the evidence of Muñoz is not conclusive without documents, and in that case the last date on which Vespucci is mentioned as being at Seville is January 12th, 1496.

10. Pliny the elder was born thirty-one years after the death of Mecænas.

11. "The sculptures of Polycletus and the paintings of Apelles." (Macaulay.)

12. Letter to Solderini, p. 3.

13. Chap. clxvi, end.

14. Letter to Medici, p. 4.

15. Letter to Solderini, Fourth Voyage, p. 53.

16. Ibid., p. 56.

17. Ibid., Second Voyage, p. 27.

18. Sebastian Cabot only knew of the qualifications of Vespucci from the report of his nephew Giovanni and others. He said, in his evidence before the Badajoz Commission (13th November 1515), that Vespucci took the altitude at Cape St. Augustine, and that he was expert in taking observations. Giovanni

Vespucci also said that his uncle took sights and kept a journal. Nuño Garcia gave similar evidence. (Extracts by Muñoz from the Registro de copias de cedulas de la Casa de la Contratacion, Nav., iii, 319.)

19. See Third voyage.

20. See Las Casas' narrative.

21. Las Casas thinks that the islands where the natives were kidnapped, called Iti by Vespucci, were Dominica and Guadalupe.

22. These dates make the voyage mentioned in an alleged letter of Vespucci, recently found in Holland, quite impossible. This fabulous voyage from Lisbon to Calicut covered the time from March 1500 to November 15th, 1501. The letter was printed in Dutch by Jan van Doesborch at Antwerp, on December 1st, 1508 (twelve leaves). Mr. Coote (in the Athenæum, Jan. 20, 1894) has suggested that the date is a mistake, and that it should be 1505-1506, the date of the Portuguese voyage of Almeida; having found that some incidents in the spurious letter occur also in the account of the voyage of Almeida. But the suggested dates are equally impossible so far as Vespucci is concerned, for he was certainly in Spain during the whole of 1505 and 1506. The letter is clearly a fabrication.

23. Nav., iii, 292.

24. Ibid., 294-95, 302.

25. See Fourth voyage.

26. Nav., iii, 299.

27. Nav., iii, 305, 308.

28. On her death, in 1524, her pension was passed on to her sister Catalina. (Nav., iii, 324.)

29. Ibid., 306.

30. See Second Voyage.

31. See Third Voyage.

32. See Third Voyage.

33. Varnhagen thought, from the places and dates of other pamphlets bound up in the same volume with his copy, that it was printed by Piero Paccini, at Pescia, in 1506.

34. The Spanish traer is used for the Italian portare four times, cansado for stanco three times, disnudi for ignudi three times, salir for escire twice, allargar for allungare twice, dismanparate for abbandonate twice, largi for lontani twice, and ruego for priego twice. Other Hispanicisms occur once, namely:—

Usado	for	Ardito.
Patagna	"	Frivolezza.
Circa	"	Vecino.
Brava	"	Selvaggio.
Dispedino	"	Licenziano.
Madiana	"	Mediocra.
Formosa	"	Bella.
Levono	"	Portano.
Vaciare	"	Votare.
Scusono	"	Ricusano.
Dolentia	"	Infirmita.
Relato	"	Raccontato.
Profito	"	Utilita.
Dimostra	"	Indizio.
Folgato	"	Spassato.
Di basso	"	Sotto.
Sabiduria	"	Sapienza.
Corregemo	"	Racconciamo.
Difesono	"	Impedirono.
Uorata in un rio.	"	Incagliata in un fiume.
Dispopolato	"	Disabitato.
Damnato	"	Damaggiato.

35. He calls a bay ensenada instead of seno, surgemo for gettamo (l'ancora), calefatar and brear instead of spalmare and impeciare, aquacero for rovescio, serrazon for oscurezza, tormento for tempesta, palo for legno, riscatto for comprato. He uses the Spanish phrase doblare un cabo, and the Portuguese word fateixa for a boat's anchor.

36. See Introduction.

37. See First Voyage.

38. See Second Voyage.

39. See Third Voyage.

40. In his second voyage he calls the cannibal tribe Cambali. Columbus, in the Journal of his first voyage, frequently mentions the Caribas or Canibas.

41. See Introduction.

42. The name of Columbus is not once mentioned in the Cosmographiæ Introductio, containing the Latin version of Vespucci. It occurs only once in the letter of Vespucci, where, in his second voyage, he mentions his arrival at Antiglia, formerly discovered by Columbus.

43. See also Navarrete, iii, 474. Peter Martyr says, "in the year before the expedition of Nicuesa and Hojeda", which was in 1509.

44. Ledesma was aged 37 in March 1513. (Nav., iii, 539.)

45. A study of Harrisse, and reference to the original authorities (after writing the note on the Pinzon and Solis voyage at p. 284 of my Life of Columbus), has led me to make several corrections, especially as regards the date of 1506 given by Herrera. The true date of the voyage was 1508.

46. Dec. II. Lib. vii, pp. 85-6, of Eden's translation (Willes' ed.).

47. "That is, the Prince of Chiauaccha, for they call princes or kings Chiaconus."

48. "The first year before the departing of the captains Nicuesa and Fogeda" (Hojeda), which was in 1509.

49. Names on the coast-line from Paria to Cabo de la Vela:—

J. DE LA COSA.	CANTINO MAP.
m. de S. eufemia.	Tamarique.
soto de uerbos.	ilha Rigua.
C. de la Vela.	boacoya.
aguada.	
lago venecuela.	golfo del unficismo.
almedabra.	
m. alto.	montansis albissima.
C. de espera.	
y. de Brasil.	ylha do Brasil.

y. de gigantes.   ylha do Giganta.
C. de la mota.   Costa de gente brava.
p. flechado.
aldea de turma.
costa pareja.   Rio de fonseca.
m. tajado.
3 echeo. Cabo de las Perlas.
Campina.   Ilha de la Rapossa.
ylhas de Sana.
G. de las Perla.   Golfo de las Perlas.
Margaleda.   terra de paria.
tres hr. I tres testigos.
boca del drago.   boca del drago.

Six of the names are the same, all the rest are different. Juan de la Cosa gives twenty-two, the Cantino map fifteen names.

50. Vespucci calls Española by the name used in Portugal—Antilla. On the Cantino map the West Indian Islands are called Antillas.

51. Dec. II, Lib. x (p. 92 in Eden's translation):—

"From the tyme, therefore, that I fyrste determined to obeye theyr requestes who wylled me fyrst in your name to wryte these thinges in the Latine tongue, I did my endevour that al things myght come foorth with due tryal and experience; whereupon I repayred to the Bishop of Burgos, beyng the cheafe refuge of this navigation. As we were therefore secretely togeather in one chamber, we had many instruments parteining to these affaires, as globes, and many of those mappes which are commonly called the shipmans cardes, or cardes of the sea. Of the which, one was drawen by the Portugales, wherunto Americus Vesputius is said to have put his hande, beyng a man most experte in this facultie, and a Florentine borne, who also under the stipende of the Portugales had sayled towarde the South pole many degrees beyonde the Equinoctial. In this carde we founde the first front of this lande to be broder then the kynges of Uraba had persuaded our men of theyr mountaynes."

52. The Viscount Santarem, principal archivist of Portugal in 1826, searched all the original correspondence of King Emanuel from 1495 to 1503 inclusive, and many thousands of documents of that time in the Torre de Tombo at Lisbon, and at Paris, but never once came across the name of Vespucci.

53. Beseneque (?).

54. A Portuguese pilot, who wrote an account of the voyage of Pedro Alvarez Cabral to India, says that on their return, on reaching the land near Cape Verde, called Beseneque, they met three Portuguese ships sent to discover the new land found by Cabral on the voyage out (Coleccion de Noticias, etc., Lisboa, 1812, cap. 21). It is very suspicious that Vespucci should not mention this meeting if he was on board one of these three ships. (Nav., iii, 310.)

55. Varnhagen supposes this land to be South Georgia, in 54° S., discovered by Captain Cook in 1776. Navarrete suggested Tristan d'Acunha.

56. Goes mentions an expedition to Brazil commanded by Gonzalo Coelho, which sailed from Lisbon on June 10th, 1503, and consisted of six ships. But Coelho returned safely with four out of his six ships, while Vespucci asserts that the commander perished, in the expedition in which he served.

57. Latin edition: "To the most illustrious René, King of Jerusalem and Sicily, Duke of Lorraine and Bar."

58. Supposed to be Pietro Soderini, Gonfaloniere of the Republic of Florence in 1504, who had studied with Vespucci. See Bandini, p. xxv.

59. Fernando is never called King of Castille in any document of the period.

60. The Latin version has 20th.

61. Inferno, Canto 26, l. 116:

"Non vogliate negar l' esperienza
Diretro al Sol, del mondo senza gente."
62. The third climate of Hipparchus
was between the parallels of Syene and
Alexandria.
63. The distance shows that, like Columbus, he reckons four miles to a
league.
64. "Ponente figliando una quarta di
libeccio." Varnhagen makes this 0¼ S.
O. A course W.S.W. for 1,000 leagues
would have taken him to the Gulf of
Paria, which is a little over 900 leagues
W.S.W. from Grand Canary. He would
not have reached land in 16° 68 N. and
70° W. even if he had steered the right
course, and there had been no intervening land, by going 1,000 leagues.
Such a distance would have left him
930 miles short of that position.
65. Twenty-seven days (Latin version).
66. Equal to 1333⅓ leagues of three
geographical miles.
67. 70° W. of Canaria, or 85° W. of
Greenwich, would be in the Pacific
Ocean; but this is a specimen of Vespucci's romancing. There was no ob-
servation for longitude with instruments in those days. Columbus observed the time occasionally, when
there was an eclipse, comparing it with
the time at some place given in his al-
manac, but the result was too rough to
be of any use.
68. The part of the mainland in 16° is
in the Gulf of Honduras. In his second
voyage he alleges that he reached 15°,
which is probably the reason why he
chose 16° for a landfall on this voyage.
69. Bombix.
70. Coltroni. Varnhagen suggests the
Spanish word colchones, mattresses;
but coltroni is a good Italian word, and
suitable.
71. Yuca is a word in the language of
the West Indian islanders for the root
of Jatophra Manihot.

72. Cazabi, the bread made from the
same root.
73. Inhame (Port.), Ñame (Sp.), a word
of African origin. Yam.
74. Zibaldone (Lat. Libellum).
75. Cani alani.
76. This is a description of the iguana,
which Vespucci would have seen on the
coast of Venezuela.
77. Lariab in the Italian edition.
78. Maestrale.
79. He says he left Cadiz on 10th May
1497. According to this it was then
10th June 1498.
80. I am indebted to Mr. Quaritch's
translation for the suggestion that the
word allogiate may be allegiate for al-
legerite ("lightened").
81. I.e., the course. Infra Greco e Le-
vante.
82. Iti (sing. Ito), an old Italian word,
meaning "gone". Here he gives it as the
name of an island. In the second voyage
he uses it for "gone"—"Dipoi che fumo
iti circa di una legua." It is probably a
name invented by himself. Navarrete
suggests it may be Ha-iti, the native
name for Española, which he adopted
for his imaginary island.
83. Two hours, in the Latin edition.
84. Latin edition has 25.
85. Both editions agree as to this number "222".
86. This is untrue. There were four
ships. See Las Casas, chap. 165.
87. He uses the word "wind" for rhumb
or course.
88. Trinidad and the Gulf of Paria.
89. Braccia is a yard, a measure of
three spans.
90. Mirabolani.
91. Alonso Niño and Cristobal Guerra,
in their voyage in 1500, observed the
same practice among the natives, and
said it was to keep their teeth white.
(Nav., iii, p. 15.)

92. Further on he says that the kinds of animals on the island were varied and numerous.

93. Iti, an old Italian word for "gone"— "Dipoi che fumo iti circa di una legua."

94. The island of Curaçoa.

95. This is untrue, as Las Casas has proved.

96. It should be 13°. The coast explored by Hojeda is, in no part, north of 13°.

97. Conta, a Portuguese word.

98. The island of Española, so called by the Portuguese.

99. September 5th, 1499, to November 22nd, 1499.

100. A false date. It should be November 22nd. He gives the day correctly.

101. These dates are shown by Las Casas to be false. Amerigo does not give any year; but the date of arrival at Cadiz was really about February 1500. Varnhagen (p. 107 n.) suggested that Hojeda and La Cosa arrived first at Española, while Vespucci remained on the coast of the mainland for some months. He refers to the evidence of one Cristobal Garcia of Palos, given on October 1st, 1515, to the effect that, he being at San Domingo, Hojeda and La Cosa arrived there in a small bark, having lost their ships, and with only fifteen or twenty men, the rest being dead (Nav., iii, 544). But this cannot refer to the voyage of 1499, when Hojeda had not lost his ships, and did not go to San Domingo. The evidence, of course, relates to his disastrous second voyage. The narrative of Roldan, quoted by Las Casas, proves that Hojeda came to Española with all his ships, that Vespucci was not left behind on the coast of the mainland, and that the dates given by Vespucci are false, either through carelessness or design.

102. Nav., iii, 544.

103. Vespucci.

104. Casas and Herrera.

105. In one of the forged letters published by Bandini. See p. 75 of Varnhagen.

106. Only mentioned in the three instructions given by Hojeda in his second voyage, to his nephew Pedro de Hojeda and Vergara to search for the vessel Santa Ana, to Vergara to go to Jamaica to buy provisions, and to Lopez to go in search of Vergara.

107. Vita del Ammiraglio, cap. 84.

108. One of the forged letters in Bandini.

109. Beze quiche, now Gorée. Biseghier in the Medici letter. Besilieca in the Latin ed.

110. S.W. ¼ S.

111. C. S. Roque.

112. "Traeua un gran palo", which is Spanish. In Italian, "portava un legno".

113. Fateixa (fatesce), a boat's anchor in Portuguese.

114. St. Augustine's Day, 28th August.

115. Lat. 26°, not 32°.

116. Verzino.

117. Varnhagen thinks this was South Georgia, so named by Cook in Jan. 1775, in 54° S. Navarrete suggests Tristan d'Acunha. Vespucci says that 50° was the furthest limit he reached to the south, along the coast, in the Medici letter, but that he then sailed to within 17° 30′ of the S. Pole, or 73° 30′ S.!! See p. 45.

118. 10th of March in the other letter.

119. This should be ten months, according to the other letter.

120. Seven days, according to the other letter.

121. 17th of August in the other letter.

122. 150 leagues, according to the other letter.

123. In the other letter he tells a very different story.

124. In 73° 30′ S.! There is no such statement in the other letter.

125. Policletus was not a painter.

126. He may mean their orbits, not the stars themselves; but in either case he is talking nonsense.

127. Zenit in the Italian version.

128. Gonzalo Coelho, according to Damian de Goez, sailed from Lisbon on an expedition to Brazil, with six ships, on June 10th, 1503.

129. This may mean either 33° S. lat.; or 33° from the Pole, which would be 57° S. lat. Malacca is in 2° 14' N. lat.

130. Fernando Noronha is probably intended.

131. Bahia.

132. If this is intended for Gonzalo Coelho, the only Portuguese commander who is recorded to have sailed from Lisbon for Brazil in 1503, the statement is false. He returned safely with four out of his six ships.

133. Navarrete, i, 351.

134. In the library of San Marco at Venice, in the books of notes of correspondence of Venetian diplomatists with the Secretary Marino Sanuto, near the end of vol. vi. (Varnhagen, Nouvelles Recherches, p. 12.)

135. Juan de la Cosa.

136. Vianelo was misinformed as to Vespucci having accompanied Juan de la Cosa on this voyage in 1506. There are documentary proofs that Vespucci was in Spain during the whole of that year. There was an intention of sending him, with Vicente Pinzon, in search of the Spice Islands by the west, and he was consulted on the subject in August 1506, but the intention was abandoned. The account given by Vianelo of the voyage (especially the stories about the dragons and the gold) may have been furnished by Vespucci. It is quite in his manner.

137. Sp., a sort of whale.

138. Vernicare, "to varnish".

139. Assassimo (?).

140. Nav., iii, 292, from the Archives of Simancas.

141. It has been pretended that John Cabot had sighted the continent in the previous year, but this is not so. He only sighted Cape Breton and other islands. In his second voyage he sighted the continent (1498), but the month is unknown.

142. Las Casas only knew the Latin version.

143. Juan de la Cosa was called "Vizcaino" (Biscayan) by his contemporaries; but he was a native of Santoña, in the province of Santander, a place which was not then, and never had been, in Biscay, or in the Basque country.

144. The words "other pilots" are to be coupled with Juan de la Cosa, certainly not with Vespucci, who then went to sea for the first time, in advanced middle age, and could in no sense be called a pilot.

145. So in the Latin edition. In the Italian version L is substituted for P, and b for s, making Lariab. This may be a misprint, but in the absence of the manuscript it is not possible to be sure whether the original word was Parias, or Lariab, or something else. Las Casas bases part of his argument on the use of the word Paria by Vespucci; but the case against the Florentine's alleged first voyage is quite conclusive, without this fact. If Vespucci did use the word Lariab, it must have been invented by him, like Iti. It is in favour of Lariab that the Italian version only passed from manuscript to print, while the Latin version was translated first into French, and thence into Latin, before it was printed. On the other hand, there is evidence that the editors of the Latin version were unacquainted with the details of the third voyage of Columbus, in which the word Paria first occurs. It, therefore, is not possible that the word can have been inserted mistakenly by them. It seems, therefore, that Lariab is a misprint of the Italian compositors, and that Parias was the word in the manuscript of Vespucci.

146. This is so. The departure, in the Latin version, is on May 20th, 1497; in the Italian it is May 10th, 1497. The date of the return is 1499 in the Latin, and 1498 in the Italian edition.

147. Columbus arrived at Santo Domingo, on his third voyage, after discovering Trinidad and the mainland of America, on August 31st, 1498. He found Francisco de Roldan in open rebellion against his brother, the Adelantado. On October 18th, 1498, he sent five ships to Spain with a cargo of dyewood, and 600 slaves. By these ships the Admiral despatched his chart of the new discoveries, with a report, and two long letters giving an account of the rebellion of Roldan and the state of the colony. Las Casas believes that letters full of complaints of the Admiral were also sent home by Roldan and his accomplices. The father of Las Casas, who had gone out with Columbus in 1493, returned to Spain by this opportunity.

148. Port of Jacmel in Española.

149. Juan de la Cosa.

150. Latin version. The Italian version has thirty-seven days.

151. Jacmel.

152. Jacmel.

153. Juan de la Cosa.

154. Puerto Rico.

155. Nav., iii, p. 558.

156. Paria.

157. Navarrete, iii, 558. Peter Martyr (Dec. I, Lib. x) says that Yañez turned his course to his left hand, by the east, to Paria, and among the princes who came to him were Chiauaccha and Pintguanus.

158. Pedro de Ledesma (being 37 in March 1513, Nav., iii, 539) was born at Seville in 1476. Gregorio Camacho heard him say that he accompanied Columbus in his first voyage (Nav., iii, 588) when he would have been aged 16. He was with Columbus in the fourth voyage, serving as a seaman in the Vizcaina, under Bartolomè Fieschi, 1503-1504, aged 27. He very gallantly swam on shore over a bar to get tidings at Veragua, but joined the mutineers at Jamaica, and was very severely wounded. In his evidence he said he was Captain and Pilot, which is false. He was pilot with Pinzon and Solis in 1510, and pilot 1511-14. He sailed with Solis to Rio de la Plata, and was drowned on the voyage home in 1516. Las Casas says he was stabbed to death in a street in Seville (iii, 180).

159. A mistake for east.

160. Lib. 11, chap. xxxix.

161. See also Peter Martyr, Dec. II, Lib. vii, p. 85.

162. In 1510, according to Peter Martyr.

163. Paria.

164. Statement of Ledesma, which is erroneous.